Battleground

FLERS
AND
GUEUDECOURT

15-26 September 1916

Battleground Europe

FLERS
AND
GUEUDECOURT

15-26 September 1916

Trevor Pidgeon

Series Editor
Nigel Cave

LEO COOPER

First published in 2002 by
LEO COOPER
an imprint of
Pen & Sword Books Limited
47 Church Street, Barnsley, South Yorkshire S70 2AS

A CIP catalogue record of this book is available
from the British Library

Printed by CPI UK.

For up-to-date information on other titles produced under the Leo Cooper imprint,
please telephone or write to:

Pen & Sword Books Ltd, FREEPOST, 47 Church Street
Barnsley, South Yorkshire S70 2AS
Telephone 01226 734222

CONTENTS

Introduction by Series Editor **6**

Author's Introduction **8**

Acknowledgements **10**

List of Maps **11**

Map Co-ordinates **12**

Advice to Travellers **14**

Chapter 1 **The Tank** **19**

Chapter 2 **The Battle Plan** **26**

Chapter 3 **15 September: 14th Division** **35**

Chapter 4 **15 September: The New Zealand Division** **56**

Chapter 5 **15 September: 41st Division** **71**

Chapter 6 **16 September: The Next Day** **102**

Chapter 7 **17-24 September: The Interval** **118**

Chapter 8 **25 September** **122**

Chapter 9 **26 September** **131**

Epilogue **136**

Index **141**

The body of a German soldier lies in a trench at Flers, September 1916. Taylor Library

Introduction by Series Editor

This battle is best known for the fact that it was the first time that a new weapon, which was to play such a significant role in the history of warfare in the twentieth century, was used. The tank made its debut appearance on the battlefield in the fields and woodlands and amongst the small villages of the Somme.

For such a momentous occasion in history, there are relatively few visitors to this particular part of the Somme. It could be that this is because there are relatively few signs – not even that many memorials – that such momentous events took place. The tank memorial is situated near the site of the windmill, on the Bapaume – Albert road, some miles' distance from Flers.

Trevor wrote what will surely be the definitive book on this action a few years ago, *The Tanks at Flers*; it is a work characterised by the high quality of production, the abundance of good, clear maps, the scouring of sources, British and German, and an intimate knowledge of the ground. He has now used this knowledge to produce this excellent survey of the actions around Flers and Gueudecourt in the last fortnight or so of September 1916. Now it is possible to put actions to the ground, as the routes of tanks are carefully laid out on maps. What seems like a typical Somme landscape of woods, huge prairie-like fields, small tractor tracks and little villages, each with their distinctive spire (but, alas, rarely with a café) is transformed into a comprehensible battlefield. The visitor to this area will be able to follow the likely routes of those tank pioneers, accompanied by the comments of those on both sides who took part in the fighting.

This battlefield is also special to me. It was here that my grandfather's brigade (110) and his battalion (7/Leicesters) saw their second major action on the Somme, after the relative success of their attack on Bazentin in mid-July. It was whilst bringing up the rations from the area of the Citadel, to the south of Fricourt, that he almost met his end when a shell fell at his feet (a dud) at Delville Wood – in fact he was only splashed all over in mud. Many of the men from 110 Brigade whom I interviewed in the early eighties described in great detail what happened here in this area which is now so peaceful and placid.

This book should go a long way to ensure that people not only know of Flers as the place where tanks were first used but can now come and visit and follow and marvel.

Nigel Cave, *Casta Natale, Rovereto.*

The church and town pond at Flers. The church was then used by Germans as a hospital.

Author's Introduction

The Battle of Flers-Courcelette, which opened on 15 September 1916, will be forever associated with the first appearance on the battlefield of tracked armour – the tank. On this day, in this one corner of France, history was made when 36 steel monsters formed up behind the British front line to attack the barbed wire, trenches and machine guns which had, until that moment, proved such a barrier – often insuperable and its capture always costly – to the Allied armies struggling to expel the invader from France. Much had been hoped of the new machine, even to the extent of seeing it as a potential 'war-winning' weapon, capable of foreshortening the slaughter and destruction which had already marked the conflict as the most disastrous in European history. This potential, however, was not realised – certainly not in 1916 – and the tank's advocates at home and in France were obliged to watch it being used, or misused, for many months to come before eventual victory. But this was a start.

For all that it was epoch-making, the tanks' presence at Flers-Courcelette did not mean that this was primarily a tank battle. Tanks were merely adjuncts to what was conceived as another infantry battle, with armour playing a subsidiary role in assisting the infantry forward. Of course, this is and has always been the role played by armour, even in later conflicts, but in 1916 the new machine's capabilities and shortcomings were insufficiently understood, its crews insufficiently trained, and new tactics insufficiently thought through for the tank to do more than offer a glimpse of its true value in war. Some men, of course, had enough imagination to foresee its wider role. These included not only the tank crews themselves but many at all levels in the Army. Even Sir Douglas Haig, all too often vilified for his allegedly short-sighted policies, was an enthusiastic supporter of the weapon. Alas certain others, some at the highest levels of command, were unwilling at first to share that enthusiasm.

Two men in particular had earlier shown vision. One was Winston Churchill who, although First Lord of the Admiralty, displayed a lively interest in terrestrial armour. His political influence in the early days of research and development of the tank was immensely important. We shall see in a later chapter how he urged the Prime Minister, Herbert Asquith, to support

Churchill as First Lord of the Admiralty.

the project, and goaded a strangely reluctant Kitchener, Secretary of State for War, into allowing the trial of a prototype machine. Confronted by War Office apathy, he thereafter conducted his own trials of experimental models, gathering together a team of Admiralty engineers who were later largely responsible for the design adopted.

The other man was Lieutenant-Colonel Ernest Swinton, an engineer and writer who, as official war correspondent at GHQ in France, saw just how great a barrier to victory was represented by trenches and wire. He was a tireless advocate of the 'machine gun destroyer' which the tank was to be. He not only lobbied for its adoption as a weapon; he recruited the men who were to man it and he set out the tactics which they were to follow. As pre-war Assistant Secretary to the Committee of Imperial Defence, he knew his way around the corridors of power. Following his spell in France he was brought back to London in the summer of 1915 and used his Whitehall experience to good effect to help bring the tank into being.

Ernest Dunlop Swinton, photographed afer promotion to the rank of major-general.

But the part played by tanks and their crews in September 1916 must not serve to conceal from us the courage, self-sacrifice, skill and devotion to duty displayed by others, whether infantry, artillerymen or airmen, and it is hoped that this book will serve, albeit in some small measure, to record the part played by all arms in fighting the great battles of September 1916 in and around Flers and Gueudecourt.[1] These two villages were at the centre of the fighting and lay on the line where the deepest penetration was planned, the capture of both being entrusted to the men of XV Corps – at various times the 14th, 21st, 41st, 55th and New Zealand Divisions. It is their operations that we discuss in this book, although three other corps were involved in the battles which stretched from Combles in the east to Courcelette in the west. For an account of their operations the reader is referred either to books in the **Battleground Europe** series or to my own earlier work, *The Tanks at Flers.*

Readers of that book will not be surprised to find some passages repeated here – we are, after all, describing more or less the same events – but clearly there has been nowhere near enough space to duplicate the detail which that earlier book contained, although in compensation more space is given here to the infantry's role and to the struggle which took place after 15 and 16 September. Additionally, the present book

1. Flers pronounced *Flair*, Gueudecourt *Gird-Koor*

will serve as a handier guide, of a size that can be carried around the battlefields by the historian, student or tourist, as he or she follows in the path of the men who fought here, suffered here or died here.

One last point. If the mention of Flers to the British conjures up a picture of tanks lumbering across the bloody fields of the Somme of 1916, to the French it has additional and slightly different connotations. For the French army was in action here much earlier in the War in an attempt – in the event unavailing – to prevent the Germans penetrating further into Picardy. It was on 26 September 1914 that the Group of Territorial Divisions commanded by General Brugère fought a bitter battle with men of the 2nd Bavarian Corps. One of those divisions, the 82nd, was tasked with defending Flers and neighbouring Ginchy. For a whole day its men kept at bay a force led by the 26th and 28th Bavarian Divisions in an engagement which caused grievous losses on both sides. Two memorials mark the event: one is the monument to the men of the 82nd Division, erected in 1934 at the southern approach to Flers itself; the other is the memorial to two men of the 18th Territorial Regiment erected beside the Flers road immediately north of Ginchy. Georges Lejoindre and Georges Pfister, together with many of their comrades, were killed near here two years to the day before a British tank carried out a spectacular and highly successful assault against those same German invaders entrenched in front of neighbouring Gueudecourt.

Acknowledgements

In writing this book, I owe much to the Tank Museum at Bovington, and especially to its Librarian, Mr. David Fletcher. His knowledge of tank history and his readiness to assist those of us attempting to chronicle it are much appreciated.

The Imperial War Museum, too, was most helpful in looking out the records and memoirs relating to the early tanks.

The staff of the Public Record Office were unfailingly kind and assisted me in many ways. The archives in their care at Kew are a treasure-house of original documents on every aspect of our nation's life.

I must thank Mrs. Mary Mortimore for allowing me to use a photograph of her husband, Captain H.W. Mortimore, and Mr. Anthony Bond for giving me the photograph of his uncle, Second Lieutenant L.C. Bond. I am also grateful to Mr. Geoff Bridger for letting me use photographs from his 'New Zealand' album and to Mr. Bob Grundy for drawing to my attention the photograph of D9 and D14.

My special thanks go to Monsieur Jean Verdel of Miraumont, whose advice, assistance and friendship I have valued over many years, and to Mr. Monty Rossiter, a tankie from 1934. He is a keen historian, an authority on the mechanism of the Mark I – and is responsible for part of Chapter 1 of this book – but above all a very good friend.

And my thanks to my wife, Marion, who has encouraged me in my researches over many years.

Cobham, October 2001

List of Maps

1 North-eastern France 14
2 The Somme battlefields of 1916 16
3 The battle front of Fourth Army 28
4 Area of XV Corps 32
5 41 Brigade of 14th Division at Zero 36
6 The Preliminary Operation 38
7 The routes taken by Head and Blowers 43
8 The later route followed by Blowers 46
9 The road to the Loop 49
10 The Loop 50
11 Green Dump 52
12 The start of the New Zealanders' attack 58
13 Later stages of the New Zealanders' attack 64
14 The start points and early progress of tanks with 41st Division 72
15 Infantry positions in 41st Division at or shortly after Zero 75
16 Later routes of the tanks with 41st Division 81
17 Legge's later route 88
18 Map drawn by *Leutnant* Braunhofer 94
19 The New Zealanders' renewed attack 103
20 The attack by 64 Brigade, 21st Division 104
21 The attack by 43 Brigade, 14th Division 108
22 Lieutenant-Colonel Ritchie's map 111
23 The New Zealanders' push north-west of Flers 119
24 The bombing raids on Point 91 120
25 The attack by 64 Brigade 122
26 The attack by 110 Brigade 124
27 The attack by 165 Brigade 127
28 The New Zealanders' push further left 129
29 Storey's attack 132

Map Coordinates

The maps used in this book are copies of British trench maps held in the Public Record Office, mostly drawn at a scale of 1:10,000 (10cms = 1km) which is about 6 inches to the mile. The map most frequently used is held in the PRO under reference WO 297 1943, and is entitled 'British Front from High Wood to Ginchy'. It is not one of the large 'Regular Series' of maps (GSGS 3062) produced by the Ordnance Survey at Southampton, but a smaller 'demy' (17½ x 22½ inches) produced in France by Fourth Army. It is printed diagonally on the sheet, a fact which may be apparent from one or two of the extracts used in this book. The date of 'trench correction' is 10 September 1916, five days before the start of the battles which we here describe, so where necessary we have added a number of trenches which were not then in existence. These are not repeated on all the extracts but only on those where the existence of such trenches was relevant to the action described in that chapter.

Other maps include 57c SW3, Longueval, edition of 29 September 1916 (a map in the Regular Series, used here to show Green Dump, lying outside the area of our main map), and one or two maps at a scale of 1:20,000 such as those of the Loop and the Battle Front, reduced to fit the format of our pages.

The maps are based on French pre-War originals, modified following a major re-survey of the ground by the British Army. These base-maps are of course metric, but in order to plot positions accurately, a system of grids was required and, because the British Army used the imperial system, its cartographers overlaid these maps with a series of squares measured in yards.

The largest squares (sometimes rectangles) commonly measure 6,000 x 6,000 yards (6,000 x 5,000 yards in the case of rectangles). This is just under 3½ x 3½ miles. Each of these large squares is identified by a letter of the alphabet. Those which concern us principally in this book are M, N, S and T.

Each large square is divided into smaller squares measuring 1,000 x 1,000 yards and numbered 1 – 36 (or 1 – 30 in the case of rectangles). In the maps shown in the chapters of this book, a place could therefore be described as lying in square N32 or in square M36.

Each of these numbered squares is further divided into four smaller squares, or sub-squares, measuring 500 x 500 yards, each of which is considered to be lettered a, b, c or d. In the example which follows, a place may therefore be described as lying in T1a or T1b. Note that only rarely are these letters shown on the sub-squares, but square S6 immediately south-west of Flers in maps 3 and 4 provides one such example.

Usually much greater accuracy is called for. For this purpose the sides of each sub-square are considered as being divided into ten. Indeed, two sides of each sub-square are actually marked off for you in this way. Count along, left to right, the number of dividing lines needed to bring you above the point in question. This is known as the 'easting'. Then count from bottom to top the number of lines required to cross the same point. This is the 'northing'. These two figures are then added to the letters and number mentioned in the preceding paragraph, e.g. T1b 8.1.

Note that these last two figures, less the full stop, are sometimes printed on the map itself as a convenient way of indicating features in enemy territory. The map used in this book provides abundant examples. One of them, Point 91 east of Flers, was to become all too well known to British troops.

The system described above gives an accuracy to within 50 yards, or 25 yards on each side of the co-ordinate specified. To give an even more precise reference, imagine that the sides of each sub-square are divided, not by ten but by one hundred. Then read off two figures for the distance left to right and two figures for the distance bottom to top. See the examples given here. This gives an accuracy of 5 yards, or $2^{1}/_{2}$ yards on each side.

Occasionally a reference is given, for example, as T1b $4.4^{1}/_{2}$ in order to provide a shade more accuracy than would be given by two figures alone. This, however, is strictly incorrect. The correct form would be T1b 40.45.

The reader will see that whereas the author has adhered to the imperial system in describing the battle – because this is used throughout the original documents – his Field Guides for those visiting the area quote all distances in metres.

One final point. The infantry positions marked on the maps are

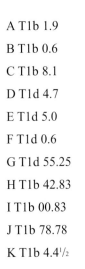

A T1b 1.9

B T1b 0.6

C T1b 8.1

D T1d 4.7

E T1d 5.0

F T1d 0.6

G T1d 55.25

H T1b 42.83

I T1b 00.83

J T1b 78.78

K T1b $4.4^{1}/_{2}$

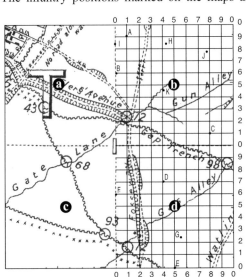

diagrammatic only. They represent the positions, as at Zero or shortly thereafter, of those battalions whose attack formations are given in their War Diaries. Only a few of these show company positions – usually A, B, C, D – while fewer still show the position of platoons.

Advice to Travellers

The area of the Somme lies just a short drive from Calais. Travellers from London, for example, can leave after breakfast and, whether by ferry or Channel Tunnel, can be in the area of the Somme by early afternoon. In the process they will have passed through or near towns and villages which have an enduring and quite unique place in British history, for this is the region of Flanders, Artois and Picardy. Exploration of these deserves a longer, much longer stay than most of us can afford. Weeks, months or even years could be spent researching the great events that swept over this ground during the years 1914-1918.

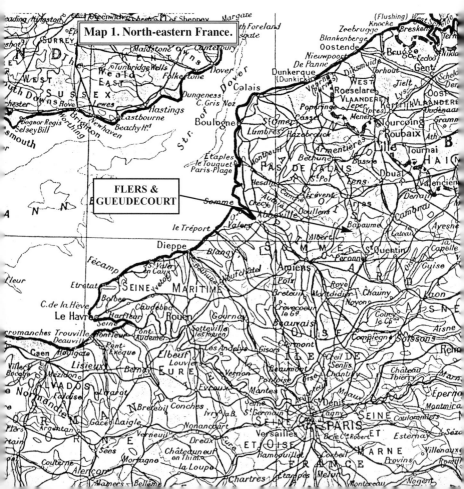

But today our destination is the area of Flers and Gueudecourt so we take the fastest route which is via Autoroute A26, turning off onto the A1 east of Arras. This in turn leads to Paris, but you, the reader of this book, will take the exit at Baupaume. Once past the toll-booth, turn left at the first roundabout onto the N29 and head for the town centre just l.25kms away. At the first major T-junction turn right – alas through heavy traffic – until you emerge after 700m where the signpost points you to the left along the D929 towards Albert. After 6 kms you pass through Le Sars (roughly where the First Battle of the Somme drew to its muddy and bloody close in 1916) then after another 2.5kms you turn off left, along the D107 signposted to Martinpuich, Longueval and the South African Memorial. Here you pass through fields which saw some of the bloodiest fighting of the whole Great War.

For those visitors wishing to stay in the area – and it has many attractions apart from its history – the author can recommend the farmhouse *gîte* of Odile and Roger Samain at the Hermitage, Grande Rue in Ginchy, 80360 (tel:00 33 3 2285 0224, fax: 00 33 3 2285 1160). This is in the heart of the tank country, but doubtless other accommodation can be had by enquiring locally or at the Syndicat d'Initiative in Albert.

Before looking at Flers and the surrounding countryside, readers of this book coming to the area for the first time may wish to spend a little while touring the other Somme battlefields nearby in order to orientate themselves. The I.G.N. maps at 1:25,000 (Série Bleue) would be excellent companions, but cheaper by far is the Michelin 1:200,000 map (no. 52 or 53), especially the edition, available locally, which is overlaid with details of the Commonwealth War Graves which are everywhere to be seen. This present book is not of course intended to be a guide, however brief, to the whole area of the Somme and we would direct readers instead to other books in the **Battleground Europe** series. But to give a rough outline: Start in the north at Foncquevillers and Hébuterne (both in British hands when the battles opened on 1 July 1916), and Gommecourt (German). Drive down to Serre and Beaumont (both German), then to Newfoundland Memorial Park, crossing the Ancre to Thiepval, Pozières and La Boisselle (all German) then to Fricourt, Mametz and Montauban (all German) and Maricourt (where the British and French stood side by side). Places featuring in later fighting included High Wood, Longueval, Le Sars and Courcelette as well as Flers and Gueudecourt, the two villages which form the subject of this book.

What is the best time to visit the Somme? Well, the author's

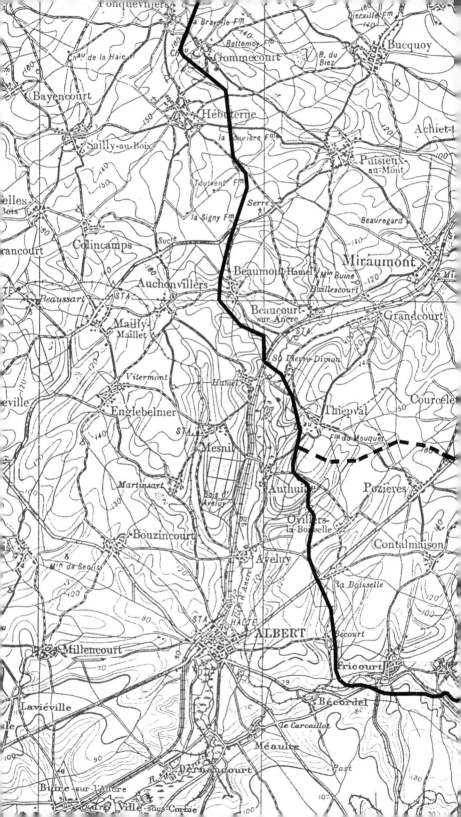

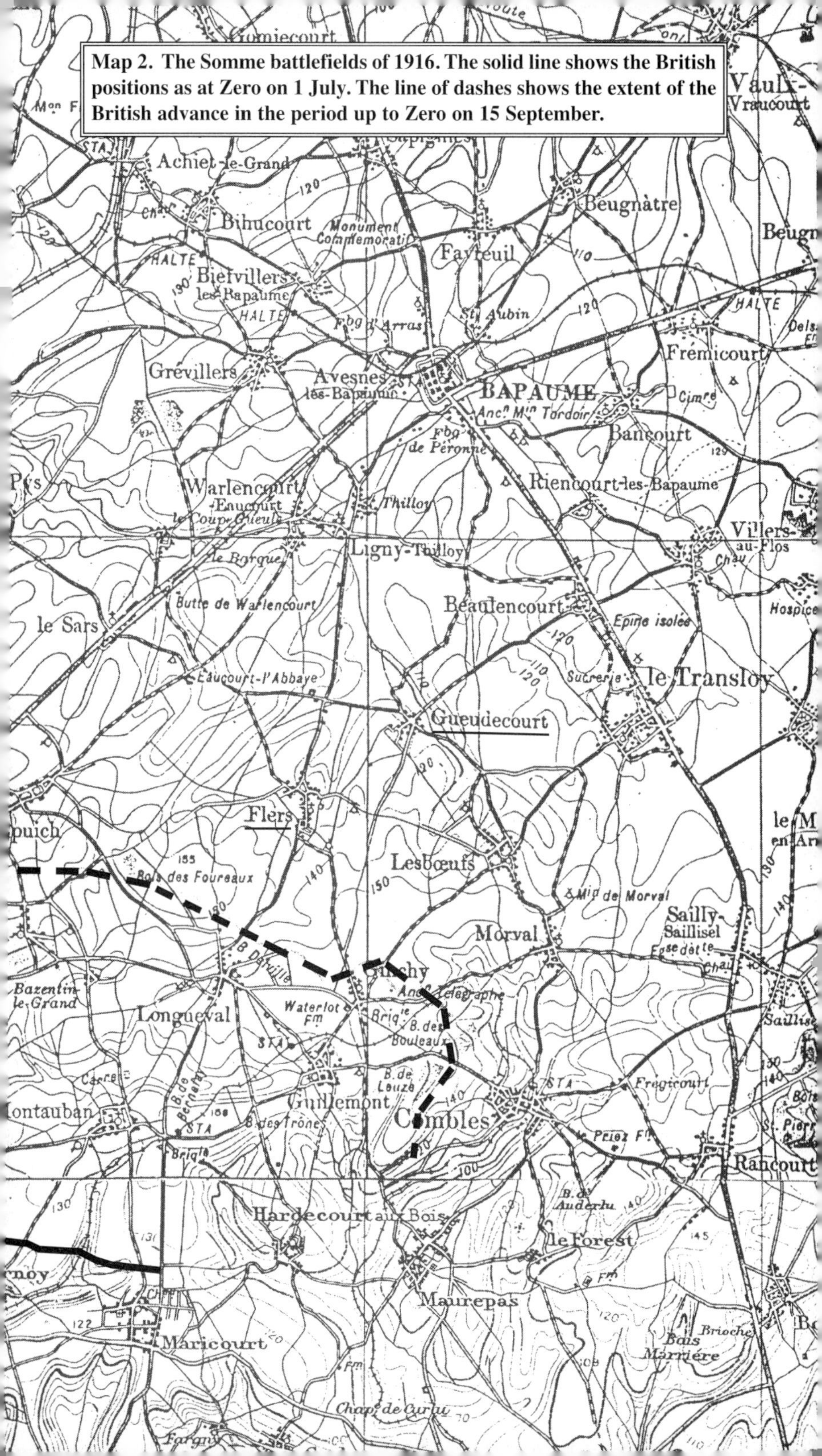

Map 2. The Somme battlefields of 1916. The solid line shows the British positions as at Zero on 1 July. The line of dashes shows the extent of the British advance in the period up to Zero on 15 September.

preference is for August when the harvest is for the most part finished and walking over the fields presents fewer problems. True, the maize can be a nuisance. At seven or eight feet high it can obscure an otherwise splendid view point until it is cut down in October. And the potato crop which here abounds has still not been gathered in. But on the whole August gives the greatest opportunity for wandering over the fields and looking at the places where the battle was fought.

This does not mean that you can wander wherever you like. The French farmer is unlikely to look kindly on you tramping over standing crops. They are, after all, his livelihood. But your polite *Bon jour* will go some way to allay his suspicions that you are bent on damaging his property. And a glance at this book in your hand will show him that you are concerned with worthy things.

August can be hot. Very hot. Wear a hat, and take an adequate supply of water. Wear good shoes or boots, for the ruts in the farm-tracks and the furrows in the fields can twist your ankle. There is much barbed wire about, old and rusting, presenting a tetanus risk. Get yourself vaccinated before you go. Above all remember that in the course of the walks described in this book you will almost certainly come across piles of shells, grenades and other material dating from the Great War. These items are still being recovered from the fields by farmers and are collected together awaiting disposal by the experts. Many prove to be live. Do not in any circumstances attempt to touch them. Injury and death are still caused many years after the battle by people who ignore this simple but essential rule.

We have provided you in this book with a number of trench maps to guide you round the battlefield, but bear in mind that although there have been fewer changes in this part of the world than in many others, the maps are not quite as accurate today as they were in 1916. In particular, years of resurfacing have made some of the many 'sunken' roads less sunken than they were. Some have acquired new importance and have been asphalted, while others have been left to decay. Some have been realigned. Some have been removed altogether but in compensation new roads have appeared elsewhere. Remember though, that 'road' was the title given in 1916 to what was often then, and is often now, no more than a rough farm-track. These tracks can be narrow, sometimes no more than two or three metres wide. Take care when parking that you do not obstruct the giant agricultural machines used throughout this part of northern France. In the event of a clash your car will undoubtedly come off worse. On the more important roads, never park on a bend. Traffic will often appear round this at quite frightening speed.

Chapter One

THE TANK

The concept of armoured vehicles has been known for centuries, as shown not just by the heavy chariots and wheeled siege-towers of ancient times, but by a whole later series of sometimes fanciful designs, put on paper but seldom translated into reality, produced by men wrestling with the age-old problem of giving an attacking force protection from the arrows, swords and gunshot of the defending enemy. A solution to the problem had to await the invention of a suitable power source, the internal combustion engine, before the concept could be turned into truly viable weapons such as those which we know nowadays as 'armoured cars'.

Vehicles such as these played an important role in Europe immediately after the outbreak of the Great War in 1914 but after the first few weeks of fighting, their usefulness, being wheeled vehicles, was found to be severely diminished by the ever-expanding system of trenches and the omnipresent, engulfing mud of Flanders. What was needed was a *tracked* vehicle which could negotiate a way through the mud and across the trenches in order to bring its fire-power up to, and through, the enemy lines.

We have already mentioned Ernest Dunlop Swinton. While no one man can be said to have 'invented' the tank, he did most to bring it into being as a viable weapon of war. As 'Eye Witness' in France in 1914 he saw at first hand the appalling cost of infantry attacks launched against entrenched troops, especially those equipped with machine guns. He recalled the tractors used over a number of years by the British Army to pull heavy artillery and those used, especially in the USA, for agricultural purposes. As an engineer, he saw these machines – their 'caterpillar' tracks giving enormous traction power and an ability to cross rough terrain – as offering the best chance of restoring a balance between attack and defence. All they needed were the guns to fight with and the armour to protect their crews.

As early as October 1914 Swinton, on leave from France, lobbied at a high level in Whitehall where he had served pre-war as Assistant Secretary to the Committee of Imperial Defence. He persuaded his former chief, Maurice Hankey, to broach the subject with the Secretary of State for War, Lord Kitchener, but the latter turned down the idea at once. In December, Hankey returned to the matter in a paper which he submitted to the Prime Minister, Herbert Asquith, who then showed it to Churchill. The First Lord of the Admiralty was enthusiastic, and scathing in his reproach to the Army for not pursuing the subject earlier. The War Office then agreed to conduct a trial with a tractor but its failure on that occasion led to no further research and the matter was allowed to drop.

But Churchill, his naval duties notwithstanding, pursued the idea. He gathered together an Admiralty team of specialists and engineers who produced a number of designs for trench-crossing machines. Some of these were fanciful, others more realistic, but none had the benefit of advice from the intended beneficiary, the Army, which kept its distance from the project.

Meanwhile Swinton, back in France, was working on a study of the mechanical and tactical problems of the 'machine gun destroyer' which he had in mind. In June 1915 he showed the document to Sir John French, the Commander-in-Chief in France, who forwarded it to the War Office. Shortly thereafter, Swinton was summoned back to London by the Prime Minister, ostensibly to resume his pre-war job at the C.I.D. in the temporary absence of Hankey, but with an opportunity, expressly provided by Hankey, to press the case for adoption of his earlier proposals. Fortunately the Army was now talking to the Navy and a prototype machine, Little Willie, was soon produced by the Admiralty team. Swinton, versed in the ways of

Prototype of the Mark I tank, affectionately known as 'Mother', on the slopes of Burton Park, Lincoln, in February 1916.

Whitehall, was made secretary of the 'Landship Committee' and used his position to good effect. When a second model, Big Willie, was adopted following trials at Hatfield in January and February 1916, he was given overall responsibility for launching the new landship, coordinating its production with the energetic Albert Stern, recruiting the men who were to man it and conducting all liaison with GHQ in France where the newly appointed C-in-C, Sir Douglas Haig, showed himself to be an enthusiastic but impatient customer.

Crews for the tanks came from a variety of sources. A number of the officers had served in the Royal Naval Air Service (RNAS), having been involved with its armoured cars from the beginning of the war. Others were infantry officers, selected in a 'trawl' of various battalions and cadet units. Some of the NCOs and men were ex-RNAS, but the larger number were recruited from the Motor Machine Gun Corps, having been made redundant, along with their motor-cycles, by the mud and trenches of Flanders. In another category were the drivers, attached from the ranks of the Army Service Corps (ASC), but the preponderance of MMGC men made it almost inevitable that they should continue to bear the MGC title and badge. They, and those coming from other units, were accordingly named the Heavy Section of the Machine Gun Corps (HSMGC), a device which helped disguise the nature of the weapon which they were to take into battle. Swinton was formally appointed to command the new formation although his duties fell short of commanding it in action in the field.

Big Willie, the Mark I tank, weighing 28 tons, was designed at the Lincoln works of William Foster & Co. by the firm's Managing

The Mark I tank. (Bovington Tank Museum)

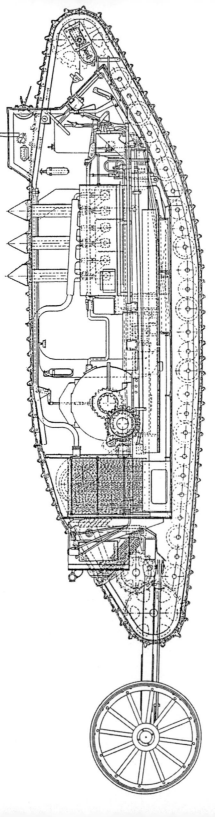

The Mark I tank: internal detail. The weight of the Mark I male was 28 tons and of the female 27 tons. The length of both was 32'6" (9.91m) with tail and 26'5" (8.05m) without. The width of the male was 13'9" (4.19m) and of the female 14'4" (4.37m). The male carried two 57mm 6-pdr Hotchkiss guns with 324 rounds, and four Hotchkiss machine guns (three mounted, plus one spare) with 6,272 rounds. The female had five Vickers machine guns (four mounted, plus one spare), one Hotchkiss machine gun and 31,232 rounds. Both versions were powered by a Daimler six-cylinder sleeve-valve petrol engine developing 105 b.h.p. at 1,000 r.p.m. The height of the Mark I was 8'0½" (2.45m) and the clearance on a hard surface 1'4⅝". (0.422m). The speeds were 0.75 m.p.h. (1.2km/h) in first gear, 1.3 m.p.h. (2km/h) in second, 2.1 m.p.h. (3.3km/h) in third and 3.7 m.p.h. (5.9km/h) in fourth. In reverse it was 0.94 m.p.h. (1.5km/h).

Director, William Tritton, and by Walter Wilson of the RNAS. It was propelled by a 105 horsepower Daimler engine and ran on linked steel tracks which encircled the entire machine, thus giving it a first-class trench-crossing capability. It was equipped with two sponsons, or turrets, bolted on to each side, these containing the main armament. This, at first, was to be the 57mm 6-pounder Hotchkiss naval gun, supplemented by Hotchkiss machine guns placed elsewhere in the tank, but it was later decided that only half the tanks – the 'males' – should be thus equipped, each sponson in the other half – the 'females' – housing instead two Vickers machine guns.

The Mark I was based on Fosters' pre-war wheeled tractor, which had only two gears. Rather than re-engineer the gearbox, which time did not allow, Wilson and Tritton added secondary gears in the hollow trackway on either side of the new machine, the high and low ratios of which gave the tank the the total of four gears which its larger weight

Often described as 'The first official picture of the Mark I tank going into action at the Battle of Flers-Courcelette', this photograph must in fact have been taken at the training ground at Elveden in England. The approach to the battle took place in darkness along roads choked with men and material. Also the ridged roof of netting shown here was an early version, abandoned long before the tanks left England, used for the experimental transmission of wireless messages. The pattern used on the tanks on 15 September was quite different. Note, however, that none of the tanks in D Company whose actions are described in this book carried the netting. Note also that the very fine photograph of a Mark I tank reproduced on page 1 is actually a C Company machine whose ridged roof of netting we have 'removed' for illustrative purposes.

D Company officers, photographed at Canada Farm, Elveden, before sailing for France. Back row, left to right: Legge, Blowers, Robinson, Bond, Bown, Drader, Bagshaw, Arnold, Hastie, Darby, Bell, Storey, Pearsall. Centre row: Colle, Enoch, Nixon, Mann?, Sellick?, Summers (Company Commander), Woods (Adjutant), Mortimore, Unknown, Wakley, Stones. Front row: Huffam, Sharp, Court, Head. The only man who fought on 15 September but is missing from this picture is Second Lieutenant W.H. Sampson.

called for. The expedient was not wholly successful, being a somewhat clumsy device calling for extra crewmen to operate it, but it met the need reasonably well in Marks I, II, III and IV throughout 1916 and 1917.

The primary method of steering in 1916 was provided by a pair of wheels trailing behind the tank as a sort of rudder, their rims pulled down into contact with the ground by means of powerful springs. Although fairly effective on flat, firm ground, the wheels were found to be much less effective on the battlefield, where they were vulnerable to shell-fire and liable to damage in the shell-holes everywhere abounding. Towards the end of 1916 they were abandoned, but not before alternative methods of steering had been explored and found to be satisfactory. The best of these was steering on the brakes , which involved braking one track in order to slew the tank round in that direction. Another method – one which allowed the tank to turn on its own axis – called for the driver to declutch, bring the tank to a halt, lock the differential, signal one gearsman to engage his low ratio, signal the other to select neutral, put his primary gearbox into low gear and, having raised his tail-wheels off the ground, engage the clutch and drive one track while the tank commander braked the one in neutral. (All this, evidently, while the enemy was busy aligning his 77mm guns to destroy both tank and crew!)

Instruction of the crews was initially given at Bisley, in Surrey, where the grounds of the National Rifle Association had for many months past been given over to training some of the thousands of infantrymen already despatched to France and Belgium. In late May and early June of 1916, the crews were transferred from there to their new base at Elveden in Suffolk, where they were soon joined by the first tanks coming off the production line. Tanks and crews were there formed into six companies – A, B, C, D, E and F – each to have twenty-five tanks, these being further subdivided into four sections each of six tanks, with one in reserve. Of the six companies sharing the hoped for total of 150 machines, it was C and D Companies that were first made ready for battle and after an all too brief period of training they crossed the Channel in August and early September.

But as we have said, we are concerned in this book primarily with the fighting on the front of XV Corps, and since it was D Company's tanks that were attached to that formation it is D Company's actions that we shall now describe.

Chapter Two

THE BATTLE PLAN

Readers of this book will no doubt be familiar with the background to the Somme fighting. Following the outbreak of hostilities in 1914 it had taken many months to increase Britain's military strength and thereafter to establish an effective presence in France and Belgium, but by 1916 she was ready to play a full part in confronting the German invader, not least in order to lessen his pressure on the French at Verdun. Her soldiers on the continent were at this stage still for the most part volunteers – amateurs thrown into a fight-to-the-death between vast professional armies – but their readiness to learn their new trade, their bravery and devotion to their cause, cannot be doubted. When the time came to launch their first truly major offensive in July 1916 they were keyed up, enthusiastic and anxious to prove their worth in combat.

Alas, their first day went badly. Stretched across 12 miles of the Somme uplands, their attack north of the Albert-Bapaume road was brought almost immediately to a standstill. The losses were horrendous. South of it, slightly better results were achieved but

New battalion for the Leicestershire Regiment taking a rest during training.
Taylor Library

The casualties of war; a soldier is helped make his way to an aid post
Taylor Library

progress here was not exploited and the day's main objectives remained for the most part as distant as they had been at Zero hour. Of almost 60,000 casualties incurred, one third were dead.

Subsequent fighting took the form of relatively small-scale but nonetheless costly operations designed to advance the British line up to the crest of the Pozières Ridge. Hopes of a major breakthrough faded, only to be revived later in the summer by the prospect of a renewed offensive which we now know as the Battle of Flers-Courcelette. Preparations began in early August, Haig putting his senior commanders on notice that the fighting was likely to reach a climax in mid-September, when a number of tanks would be available to assist an advance. This would be designed to capture the German defences between Morval and Le Sars 'with a view to opening the way for the cavalry'.

General Sir Henry Rawlinson, who as commander of Fourth Army was the man most closely involved in carrying out Haig's instructions,

British dead awaiting identification and burial. Taylor Library

Map 3. The battle front of Fourth Army, 15 September 1916. The original map (WO 158 330 in the PRO) is on a scale of 1:20,000 here reduced to 55%. Each numbered square measures 1,000 x 1,000 yards, each smaller square 500 x 500 yards. Just visible are the original

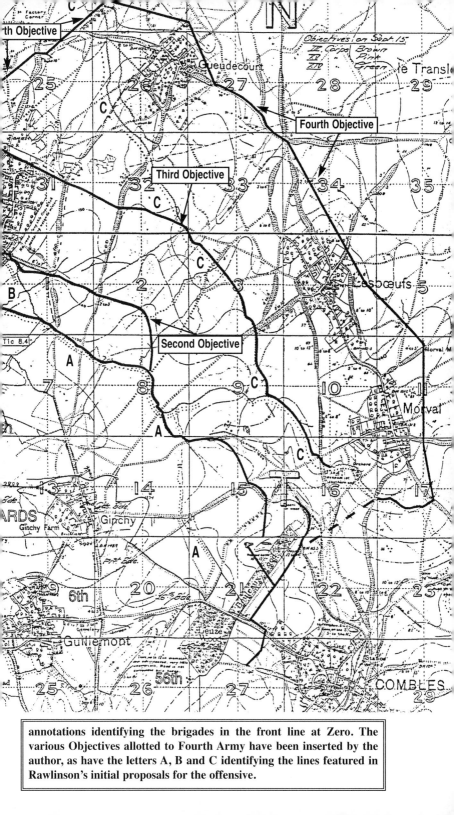

annotations identifying the brigades in the front line at Zero. The various Objectives allotted to Fourth Army have been inserted by the author, as have the letters A, B and C identifying the lines featured in Rawlinson's initial proposals for the offensive.

submitted a plan whereby the tanks would attack by night, their role being to place the infantry securely on the Germans' first major defence line (A on our map). This passed through Bouleaux Wood, threaded its way south of Flers, then through High Wood to Martinpuich. By withdrawing before dawn their secret would be kept intact and they could thus repeat the exercise the following night by returning to attack and 'roll up' a second trench (B) which branched off from (A) towards Le Sars. The third night would see a similar assault on the Germans' next line of defence (C), known to them as the *Gallwitz Riegel*, south and west of Gueudecourt.

Haig did not like this plan and called for one based on much bolder action. The concept of using the tanks at night was dropped (even though Haig's own headquarters had endorsed the idea earlier on) and a more powerful assault was to be made in daylight, its purpose being to establish a defensive flank facing east between Morval and Bapaume, while projecting a main thrust to the north aimed at cutting off the German salient near Serre.

All arrangements are to be made with a view to overwhelming the enemy at the outset by a powerful assault and following up every advantage gained with rapidity and vigour. The exploitation of success to the full during the first few hours is essential to a decision and it must be impressed on all Corps and Divisional Commanders that the situation calls for great boldness and determination on their part. It lies with them to feel the pulse of the battle and to turn favourable opportunities at once to the fullest account. In particular it is of great importance to reach the enemy's artillery positions quickly and capture his guns. Risks must be minimised not by declining to accept them but by skilful handling of reserves. The necessity for great vigour and determination in this attack, and the great results that may be achieved by it, must be impressed on all ranks as soon as considerations of secrecy will permit of their being informed of what is required of them. It will also be necessary then to impress on all leaders that the slow methods of trench warfare are unsuited to the style of operations they will be called on to undertake after the enemy has been driven from his prepared lines of defence.

This was clearly to be an an ambitious operation. Rawlinson of course complied with the Commander-in-Chief's wishes and submitted revised proposals setting Sapignies, Achiet-le-Grand and Miraumont as the targets for the main thrust. He also specified the first day's four

'Objectives' – lines on the map, in most cases identical with enemy trenches or natural features, which the artillery was to bombard and the tanks and infantry subsequently to assault as the advance progressed.

Each arm – artillery, cavalry, tanks and infantry – was given its own instructions. As far as the first of these was concerned, their task was not simply to provide the complex barrage programmes to prepare for and support the advance at Zero but thereafter to push guns and ammunition as far forward as necessary to keep pace with the infantry's progress and thus to keep the retreating enemy within range. It was therefore necessary for battery commanders to select likely firing positions beyond the present battle line, and to determine the best routes for reaching them. When the time came to move forward, artillery units were to be given every assistance from infantry and cavalry to reach their new positions.

The five cavalry divisions, for their part, were to assemble well behind the lines to await the call forward. Two of these were posted in the Carnoy-Mametz area, another near Dernancourt, one north of Bray, and one near Bonnay, nine miles south-west of Albert. Their initial objective, once the enemy's defences were broken and his nearer

Cavalry lines on the Somme, September 1916.

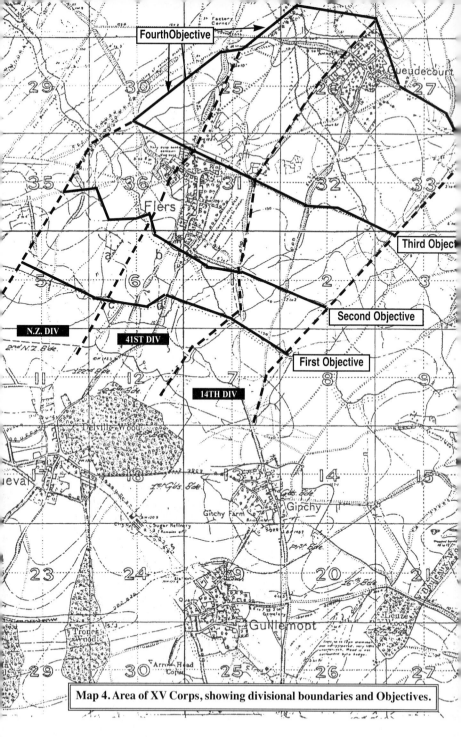

Map 4. Area of XV Corps, showing divisional boundaries and Objectives.

batteries overrun, was to be the high ground between Rocquigny and Bapaume, which the infantry were then to consolidate. Thereafter they were not only to assist those other infantry units engaged in the northward thrust but also to send out strong patrols and raiding parties to disrupt German command and supply posts well to the east – Etricourt, Vélu, Epehy (11 miles east of Combles) and incredibly even Marcoing (13 miles east of Bapaume).

As for the tanks, Rawlinson discussed the options with his most senior officers, but these had a less than perfect grasp of the capabilities and shortcomings of the new weapon and the debate was less fruitful as a result. Nonetheless, instructions were issued by Fourth Army on 11 September, laying down the necessary orders for assembly and attack. Moving off from their base at the Loop, near Bray, in the late afternoon of X day (13 September) they were to arrive at their various points of assembly a mile or so behind the lines during the night X/Y. Final preparations for the battle were to be made during Y day (14 September), then during the night Y/Z they were to take up battle positions near the front line. During both nights RFC aircraft were to fly over enemy lines to mask the noise of the tanks' motors. The question of camouflage to protect the tanks from air observation on Y day seems to have been left to individual commanders to decide, but it should be remembered that at this stage of the war Britain had air superiority over the Germans.

Fourth Army laid it down that generally the tanks were to start movement at a time so calculated that they would reach the First Objective five minutes before the infantry. In some instances however, they were specifically instructed to reach it at 6.18 a.m., two minutes before Zero. In both cases this was so that the tanks' machine guns might keep the Germans' heads down as the attacking infantry began their advance across the open space of No Man's Land.

Only a limited amount of time had been spent debating the new tactics which the new weapon required. Most of the original thinking on the subject had been done by Swinton back in February, and indeed in the previous summer, when he had suggested that the tanks should advance in single line abreast. This principle was endorsed by Haig's staff at a meeting with Swinton in London on 26 June but when Rawlinson discussed the question with his senior officers in France as late as 5 September he proposed that the tanks should advance instead in a diamond pattern of four. This was subsequently amended to groups of three, in single file ahead, but still a short distance in front of the infantry, as Swinton had proposed. In doing so, they would of course be that much closer to – perhaps even *inside* – the creeping barrage, so it was agreed that this should fall only on the ground in between each group. This would leave 'lanes' (as they were later called) in the barrage through which the tanks could advance in safety. In the event, this neat arrangement was subject to further modification, in large part dictated by individual circumstance and the fortune of battle. Tanks were used in groups, or singly, as determined by breakdowns, ditching and casualties. And the lanes were sometimes not used, simply because the tanks did not get far enough forward. This left the German defenders there untouched by the barrage.

Haig himself had suggested that, when the infantry arrived at the First Objective (usually several hundred yards beyond the German front trenches, and more logically called the first *pause* line or first *target* line), and when the artillery barrage had 'lifted' from this to its next target, certain of the tanks should take up position a short distance ahead in order to prevent any German infantry manning the next trenches from harrassing the British infantry while these were busy re-forming. This procedure was to be repeated at later Objectives.

The instructions described the speed of the tanks, over heavily shelled ground, as being not much more than 15 yards per minute. This might be increased to 33 yards over good ground and to 50 yards over good ground downhill. This of course was not fast, hence the requirement that the infantry should on no account wait for the tanks if these were to lag behind.

Finally, infantry staff were ordered to give every assistance to tank officers, who were without exception unfamiliar with the ground and with the conditions of the battle. Their brief visits to the front line on 14 September to survey the ground over which they were to take their tanks on the morrow did little to improve their knowledge of the hazards ahead, except perhaps by showing them just how lacking in landmarks and other points of reference the shell-torn landscape was.

The day's tasks were clearly not going to be achieved easily.

Chapter Three

15 SEPTEMBER
14th Division

14th (Light) Division had been in France since May 1915. It was quickly plunged then into bitter fighting at Bellewaarde and Hooge near Ypres but now on the Somme it faced an equally daunting trial, made more hazardous by the presence on its flank of a deep enemy salient which cut back between 14th Division and their neighbours in the Guards Division to the east. This was the Brewery, so-called because of the trenches – most of them still held by the Germans, but some now absorbed into the British lines – which occupied the area between Delville Wood and Ginchy. These were Beer, Ale, Hop, Lager, Stout, Bitter, Pilsen, Porter, Pint, Vat. The danger which they presented was clear. When the British on either side moved forward at Zero, the German machine guns in the Brewery would have superb enfilade targets and could bring to a halt the whole advance in this sector. They had already blocked earlier British attempts at penetration here.

Lieutenant-General Horne, commanding XV Corps, was understandably anxious to avoid such an eventuality and his concern was shared by Lieutenant-General Lord Cavan, commanding XIV Corps to his east, where the Guards Division was to advance north-east from Ginchy on the far side of the salient. Horne decided to send two tanks into the area before Zero in a 'Preliminary Operation' designed to destroy any enemy found there. A third tank was to be sent in by the Guards Division.

The 14th Division was deployed along the Longueval-Ginchy road and out into the fields to the north of Delville Wood. In between the two groups, more men lay waiting in trenches and shallow pits inside the wood but they had avoided its easternmost edges in the belief that German troops from Ale Alley had maintained a finger-nail grip on the wood's extreme tip where Ale Alley abutted it.

The leading troops at Zero were to be 8/Rifle Brigade and 8/King's

**eutenant-General
Lord Cavan**

**Lieutenant-General
Horne**

35

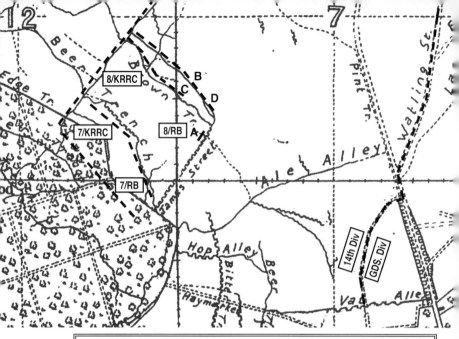

Map 5. 41 Brigade of 14th Division at Zero. The front-line troops were in Brown Trench, the supporting troops in Delville Wood and in Green Trench, formerly Beer Trench (as on our map). The change of name here must have taken place shortly before the battle and was possibly prompted by the need to distinguish this trench from the other Beer Trench further east. However, given that the names Green Line and Brown Line were already allotted to the First and Second Objectives, the confusion may have been made worse.

Royal Rifle Corps, most of the men now concealed in Brown Trench and in a recently dug parallel trench 75 yards ahead. The men of A Company of 8/Rifle Brigade were in James Street, facing south-east towards the Brewery but ready to move up to Brown Trench before Zero in support of D Company's north-easterly advance. Waiting in Green Trench (formerly Beer Trench) and in trenches in Delville Wood were 7/Rifle Brigade and 7/KRRC. Together these four battalions made up 41 (Greenjacket) Brigade.

(The reader may well be confused by these titles, for the Rifle Brigade was not a brigade in the sense used here and elsewhere in this book, i.e. a formation and level of command normally consisting, like 41 Brigade, of four battalions; nor was the KRRC a corps, i.e. a level between division and Army. Both were *regiments*, comprising several battalions.)

The British front line along the Longueval-Ginchy road (known as South Street to the British) was held by a company of 6/King's Own

Yorkshire Light Infantry, sheltering in the trench known as Pilsen Lane which followed the road's northern edge. Another company lined the nearer edges of Delville Wood, just below where it was thought the Germans could be holding out. Both were attached from 43 Brigade, the remainder of which was held in reserve in the rear. Nearer to hand, in and around the valley south-west of Longueval, 42 Brigade waited its turn to take part in the battle.

The 14th had been ordered to advance in a north-easterly direction with the object of attacking and capturing Gueudecourt lying 1,500 yards (1,400m) beyond the north-east corner of Flers, in other words 4,400 yards (4,000m) beyond the division's start point at Delville Wood. The route of the attack would take the division alongside the eastern edge of Flers where their presence would lend support to troops on their left, pushing up inside the village itself. In the course of the division's assault, men of its 41 Brigade were to capture the first two Objectives, the second two being captured by 42 Brigade.

Zero was to be at 6.20 a.m. but before this the tanks allocated to the Preliminary Operation were to go into action. The two machines from 14th Division were D1, the first tank in the Heavy Section's D Company, commanded by Captain Harold Mortimore, and D5, Dolphin, commanded by Second Lieutenant Arthur Blowers. Of these, Blowers was to make his way through the wreckage of Delville Wood in order to reach its northern face by 5.00 a.m., at which time he was to set out to attack Brewery Salient from the rear. Mortimore was to attack it from the south, setting out at 5.10 a.m. Both were then to move north-east in support of the infantry.

Blowers negotiated the wood as best he could but the smashed trees and jagged stumps must have been a nightmare for him and his driver. Dolphin fell into a shell-hole, broke its tail-wheel assembly and was

Wreckage of Delville Wood through which Blowers drove his D5. Taylor Library

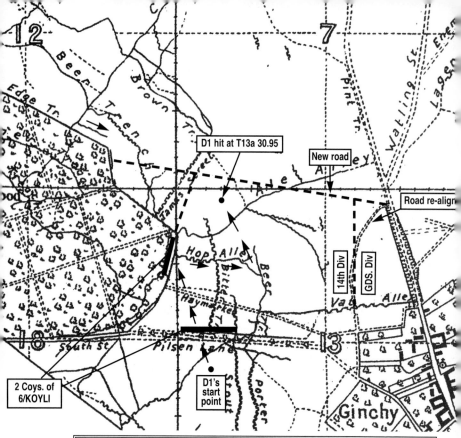

Map 6. The 'Preliminary Operation'. The world's first tank to go into action – Captain H.W. Mortimore's D1 – left its start point 100 yards south of the Longueval - Ginchy road at 5.15 a.m. on 15 September 1916. Its targets were the German trenches in the 'Brewery Salient'.

immobilised. Fortunately another tank (see below) was on hand to help extricate the machine and, by raising the tail off the ground, Blowers got it going on its path once more, albeit with limited steering. But the delay was too long to enable him to join Mortimore at the Brewery. Mortimore was now on his own.

During the night, he had moved up from Bernafay Wood to his departure point 100 yards south of the Longueval-Ginchy road. He then set out, still in darkness, at 5.15 a.m., just five minutes late. In doing so he became the first man in the world to take a tank into battle. All the tanks that have ever operated anywhere in the world since this day follow, in a sense, in the path of D1. Those at Cambrai in 1917, those in France in 1940, in the Western Desert, on the Russian steppes,

Captain Harold Mortimore, of the Heavy Section, Machine Gun Corps, the first man to command a tank in battle. (Courtesy of Mrs. Mary Mortimore.)

in Normandy and elsewhere, all these must look to D1 as their forebear.

Grinding his way along a taped lane, with a man in front guiding his progress by means of luminous disks, Mortimore took D1 over the road and through the waiting KOYLI who parted to let its shadowy bulk pass into No Man's Land beyond them. Here there was no guide and no tape but at least it was gradually getting light. The wilderness of stumps that marked the outline of Delville Wood could now just be seen, then later the place where the German trenches abutted the trees. This was Mortimore's target. He fired his 6-pounder guns at the wood, presumably satisfying himself that he had destroyed the enemy lurking there, and then turned right along Hop Alley.

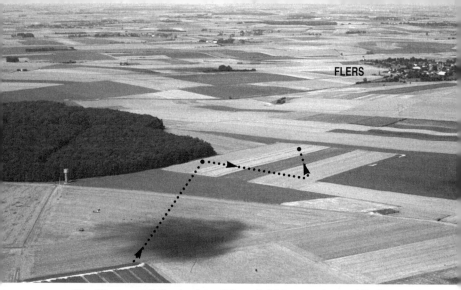

FLERS

The 'Brewery' Salient, where D1 made history as the world's first tank to enter battle. Commanded by Captain H.W. Mortimore, it set out an hour and five minutes before Zero to cross the Longueval-Ginchy road and clear the enemy out of trenches threatening the British advance on 15 September 1916. (TP 1993)

At 5.30 a.m. W and X Companies of 6/KOYLI commanded by Major W.H. Charlesworth rose up out of Pilsen Lane and broke out of the wood in order to join Mortimore in the attack. He turned left at the junction with Beer Trench and then crossed Ale Alley, clearing out the few remaining Germans as he went and firing on those fleeing to the north-east.

He did not get far. A shell landed nearby and put D1 out of action – whether by damaging the tail-assembly or the rear sprocket and track is not clear. The set-back was made all the more regrettable in so far as the shell was probably British! Mortimore had been warned not to get too far forward, and stray into the British barrage which here was very ragged (worn buffer springs on the guns were blamed) but he had done so, either because he was anxious to get to closer grips with the enemy or because he was looking for the missing Blowers on the north side of the wood.

The tank was now useless but by clearing the Brewery it had at least served to avoid what could have been a very dangerous situation for 14th Division. Also for the Guards whose own tank C24, Clan Cameron, had arrived too late to join in the fight.

As for the other tanks with 14th Division, Second Lieutenant Head in D3 was to go through Delville Wood in order to set out along Cocoa Lane, the division's west boundary, at 5.27 a.m. He was delayed by the need to help Blowers out of the shell-hole and then to negotiate his way over a pile of live mortar shells that he found blocking his path, but he eventually managed to get there. It had been intended that he should be accompanied by Second Lieutenant C.E. Storey in D4, but Storey ditched inside Delville Wood and took no part in the day's events. His moment of glory was to come eleven days later, on 26 September.

Artillery support for this offensive had been assembled on a massive scale during the previous days and on 12 September had begun a programme of bombardment of the enemy trenches. This took the form of night-time shelling up until 6.00 a.m., followed by more intense fire thereafter, but on 15 September a much greater concentration of fire was unleashed by the guns at Zero hour, 6.20 a.m. A 'stationary' barrage was put down on the First Objective while a 'creeping' barrage – one of the shells from which almost certainly knocked out Mortimore's D1 – crashed down just in front of the British lines. At the same moment, the whistles blew and the men of 41 Brigade moved to the assault. Leading waves of 8/Rifle Brigade on the right and 8/KRRC on the left set out at a steady pace, following the barrage as closely as they could as it moved ahead, leading them first down into the shallow valley of No Man s Land then across towards the German trenches. A second wave of men followed, while in the rear their comrades in 7/Rifle Brigade and 7/KRRC emerged from the wood to join the advance.

> *That advance was a sight that will live in one's memory for ever. It might have been an ordinary peace manoeuvre on Laffan's Plain* [near Aldershot]. *The long, thin lines of men, for as far as one could see to left and right, walked steadily on, their dressing almost perfectly even.*

Casualties were at first not severe. The British artillery programme before Zero had been similar to that on previous days and the Germans may have been deceived into thinking that the guns would soon switch, as before, to a reduced rate of fire. But the unexpected increase of fire and the appearance of wave after wave of advancing Tommies quickly dispelled any such illusion and the defending machine gunners and riflemen rapidly manned their posts lining Pint Trench (the embankment of the Ginchy-Flers road) and Tea Support.

> *Our first line at once instinctively moved forward at the double, getting in with cold steel, but unfortunately coming under our own barrage for a moment while doing so, which was certainly less costly than being mown down by machine gun fire – a choice of two evils perhaps, of which they chose the right*

one... [From Tea Support] they went steadily up the hill, at the top of which was Switch Trench. At the forward crest of the hill more of the enemy were met with, who gave us considerable trouble, and cost us some valuable men, but there was no faltering, and these were got rid of by the same process as at Tea Support. Once on the crest, there was found to be a plateau some 200 yards across, which came as a surprise, being difficult to see on the map, and Switch Trench was in about the centre of it. We had some difficulty finding it, so knocked about was it, and the enemy wire did not exist at all. We did not come across a piece longer than a foot anywhere.[i]

The view from Switch Trench is worthy of mention. We could see for miles, and Bapaume... .stood out in the distance. Nearer lay Gueudecourt, which was our division's objective, Flers to our left front, and Les Boeufs to our right front. During the afternoon we saw a German counter-attack on our forward line rolled up, but if everything we saw from this vantage point were to be put into this account it would never be finished.

The Germans at Pint Trench and Tea Support should of course have been quickly dealt with by the tanks but, in the right-hand sector at least, they were nowhere to be seen. Mortimore's D1 was out of action and Blowers' D5 was delayed in getting clear of Delville Wood. The commander of the Guards Division tank, C24 (Clan Cameron), one of whose tasks was to attack Pint Trench and subdue a machine gun sited at its junction with Tea Support, was confused by the conflicting orders issued to him and did not go far enough forward in time. In any case his tank was already damaged.

The infantry suffered in consequence, most of the casualties being sustained by 8/Rifle Brigade on the right. The men in 8/KRRC on the left fared better, partly because there was no enemy defence-work on their flank, like Pint Trench, but mainly because they had a tank with them – Head's D3 – which preceded them across No Man's Land in precisely the manner laid down in its orders. But progress through the chaos of shell-holes here was not easy. Not a landmark was to be seen, and Cocoa Lane itself was unrecognisable as a trench. No wonder then that D3 wandered off to one side, and when it was hit by a shell, or a fragment of shell, that crippled its steering it was able only to limp across to the shelter of an embankment in the neighbouring division's sector. Men of the Army Service Corps (ASC) attempted to recover it but several days had to elapse before this became possible. The anonymous KRRC historian ('Chronicles') makes no explicit

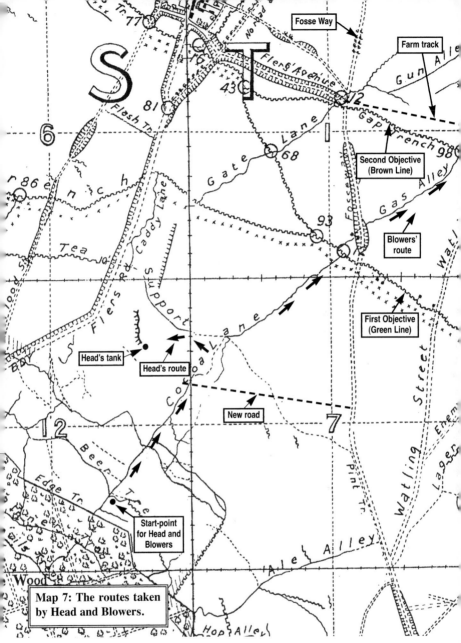

Map 7: The routes taken by Head and Blowers.

reference to Head's D3 but says merely:

> This was the first time that the tanks had been in action. I do not here intend to enlarge upon their great powers...It is sufficient to say that they were of the greatest use in the attack.

Eventually Blowers, too, was ready for action. Clearly too late to help Mortimore in the Brewery over on the right, he decided to advance straight down Cocoa Lane on the left and catch up the leading waves of infantry as best he could. At a point just short of the German front line in Tea Support he would have seen tank D3 disabled on his left and would have realised that Head had veered away from the actual course laid down. So he carried straight on, along Cocoa Lane and up to the First Objective or Green Line. This was now virtually obliterated but here the leading waves of infantry had begun tending their wounded, counting their dead, and re-forming their survivors. After a brief pause Blowers continued his north-easterly path, now along Gas Alley, across the Ginchy-Flers road and up to the Second Objective or Brown Line, where the battalions of 41 Brigade were being relieved by those of 42 Brigade.

Again, Blowers paused here only briefly before setting out once more, this time for Watling Street, the British name for the Ginchy-Gueudecourt track or *Chemin des Guilmonniers*. His actual orders were that he should cross this, then continue along Gas Alley for 400 yards before swinging back onto Watling Street, but the purpose of this proposed detour remains obscure and Blowers, no doubt anxious to make up for lost time, probably chose to ignore it, or at least to foreshorten it. Thereafter, he stuck closely to Watling Street which here becomes progressively deeper, causing Blowers to remain up on its eastern lip.

Having begun the attack on a fairly narrow front, 14th Division's sector had now broadened out. From the First Objective, where it was only 650 yards wide, it had expanded to 1,000 yards at the Second Objective (Gap Trench). From now on it was gradually to widen even further to reach as much as 1,500 yards at the Third Objective (Bulls Road) lying ahead. The men of 42 Brigade – 9/Rifle Brigade and 5/King's Shropshire Light Infantry in front, followed by 9/KRRC and 5/Oxfordshire and Buckinghamshire Light Infantry – had suffered casualties even before arriving at Gap Trench. Now, leading the attack, they suffered more, but the widening front and consequent thinning of their formation may have saved them from even greater losses, especially east of Watling Street, where a German machine gun or guns at Point 91 in Gird Trench on their right front had already inflicted much damage, especially on the Rifle Brigade and particularly on their officers.[ii]

Peering ahead through the visor of his tank, Blowers would not have been aware of this for he was now ahead of most of the infantry. But

Germans man a 77mm field gun, the type used by 1/Battery, 7/Saxon Field Artillery Regiment.

not all. Parties of men had already pushed forward on either side of, and inside, the sunken course of Watling Street. They had attacked two German cannon – 77mm field guns belonging to the Sunken Road Section (*Hohlwegzug*) of 1/Battery, 7/Saxon Field Artillery Regiment, positioned just south of the junction with Bulls Road. In the encounter they had taken the full force of case-shot from these guns, commanded by *Leutnant* Kohl, son of a German general. Despite their losses, men of 9/KRRC under the command of Sergeant Elderfield, supported by machine guns further back, crept forward close enough to pick off the crews. Others escaped, and in the end only Kohl and a few of his men were left to defend themselves with small arms fire. They finally disabled the guns and fled, but Elderfield's men shot Kohl before he had gone ten yards. Gravely wounded, he was dragged 200 yards along Watling Street by his companions before they abandoned him to die.

Elderfield and his party pursued them northwards, reportedly as far as Gird Trench, but must now have become conscious of the lack of support being given by their own side. The few men still around them, both Rifle Brigade and KRRC, were thinning out, their ranks still subjected to withering fire from the machine guns at Point 91 and elsewhere in Gird Trench to their east. Worse still, the British barrage here which was supposed to assist the advance was a poor affair, hardly a barrage at all. Heavy guns were still firing but the field guns were strangely quiet, possibly because – despite the instruction in Operational Orders – the batteries had not been advanced far enough

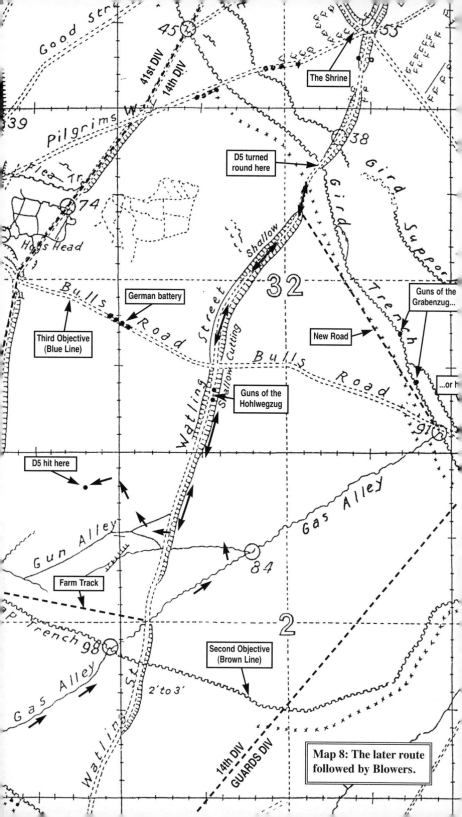

Map 8: The later route followed by Blowers.

forward in time to assist the leading units with accurate fire.

Track marks shown in air photographs taken later by the Royal Flying Corps, e.g. 9c 1872 of 23 September, indicate that Blowers followed Watling Street as far as the point where it was crossed by Gird Trench. Here he turned round. The infantry had now withdrawn and Blowers, on his own, could not risk entering an area where heavy shells were falling, however sporadically. All tank commanders had been warned, after all, not to allow their machines to fall into enemy hands. He was almost certainly aware also that the German battery whose two *Hohlwegzug* guns he had just passed, had positioned its two other guns, the *Grabenzug*, in Gird Trench to his right. So he turned and headed south, no doubt thankful that the crews of these guns were still keeping their heads down. Machine guns, of course, presented less of a problem for Dolphin.

He passed back down Watling Street, over the Bulls Road junction, moving again to the eastern lip of Watling Street to avoid being boxed in by the high sides. At some point he was met by a runner, possibly from 5/King's Shropshire Light Infantry, who asked him to support the attackers nearer to Flers. Blowers agreed, but would have had to travel a full 500 yards south of Bulls Road to find a suitable place to cross over to the western side of Watling Street. Having done so, he

The field east of Flers where tank D5, Dolphin, was destroyed. Late in leaving Delville Wood, Blowers passed the First, then Second Objectives before following Watling Street (Chemin des Guilmonniers) as far as the Third Objective at Bulls Road. He then pressed on further to Gird Trench, but when he saw that the infantry had not followed him, he was forced to re-trace his path. Answering a call for assistance he crossed over to the west side of Watling Street but was then hit by shellfire from a German battery on Bulls Road. (TP 1993.)

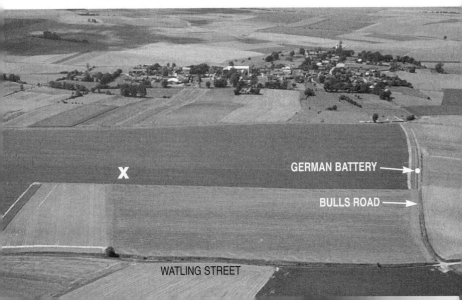

The wreck of Dolphin, its track marks still visible. The light object is the tank, the dark area its shadow. All around are the paths made by infantry. (Magnified portion of IWM photograph 9c 1872 taken on 23 September)

manoeuvred for the attack but as he was crossing the fields east of the village Dolphin was hit by one of the guns of a second German battery, sited in Bulls Road. Two of the tank's crew were killed, the rest wounded.

Blowers was awarded the MC. His second in command, Corporal Edward Foden, and his driver, Private G.H. Thomas of the ASC, both received the MM. Having started late, Blowers' tank had travelled further than any other machine on this day – 4,800 yards (4,400m) from the northern edge of Delville Wood to the point where it was destroyed. He had not reached the Fourth Objective, nor even the outskirts of Gueudecourt (as D Company papers seem to claim), but he *had* reached the Gird Line just south of the village and had supported the infantry attack with dash, courage and determination, allowing them to penetrate the enemy defences to a considerable depth. That was a notable achievement on this, the first day of the tanks.

Without his support, the infantry here could not go further. They overwhelmed the enemy battery on Bulls Road but were obliged to dig in on a line just south of the road.

Field Guide

All the tanks operating with XV Corps assembled in the first instance at the Loop, an area enclosed by the pre-War metre-gauge railway line from Fricourt to Bray-sur-Somme, which negotiated its drop into the *Vallée Raison* by describing a tight bend in the fields not far from Bronfay Farm, itself well-known to the men of 1916. From Bray, take the D329 north, but immediately out of the town turn right onto the D147 signposted to Fricourt. After no more than 200m ignore the leftward bend and carry straight on. After 2km the road rises between scrubby trees. Where it flattens out on the top was where the railway once crossed over to the right to begin the *Fer à Cheval* (the Horseshoe, known as the Loop to the British).

The tanks allocated to XV Corps left the Loop on the evening of 13 September to proceed via Montauban to their next stop which was Green Dump, near Longueval. All except one, that is. Harold Mortimore's D1 was singled out and directed to a point just north of Bernafay Wood, there to await orders for its further advance. The others took the road which now turns right, alongside the north wall of the C.W.G.C.'s Quarry Cemetery outside Montauban, then climbed up

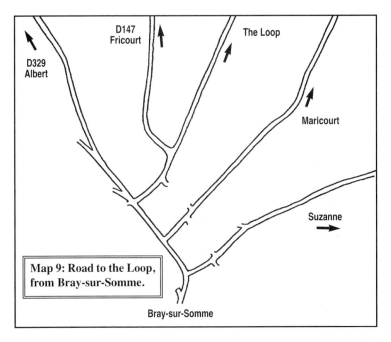

Map 9: Road to the Loop, from Bray-sur-Somme.

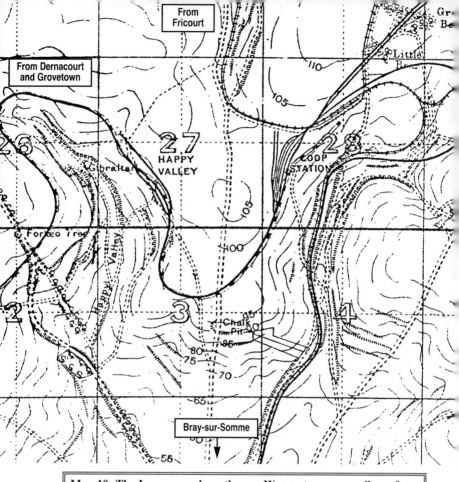

From Fricourt

From Dernacourt and Grovetown

HAPPY VALLEY

LOOP STATION

Gibraltar

Forked Tree

Chalk Pit

110

105

105

100

85

80

75

70

65

60

55

Bray-sur-Somme

Map 10: The Loop was where the pre-War metre-gauge railway from Fricourt wound its way down into the Vallée Raison on its way to Bray-sur-Somme. In 1916 a British-built standard-gauge line from Dernancourt was brought up to this area via Grovetown and Happy Valley (important transit points for infantry) to form an unloading place for supplies, and eventually for tanks. Later, as the battle progressed, this 'Plateau Line' was extended and expanded, as shown here, but in early September its role was to off-load almost all the tanks that were to be employed in the battle, with the exception of those supporting the 2nd Canadian Division near the Albert-Bapaume road. Alas, the line of hedges which until recently marked the curve of the Loop has now been ploughed under, as have the sidings of Loop Station where the tanks were delivered. But in those last few days before the battle in September 1916 the Loop and the valley leading down to Bray saw enormous activity. Here came senior officers of all arms to watch the machines perform, and here the tank men spent what little time they were allowed in order to tune, grease and equip their machines for the struggle ahead.

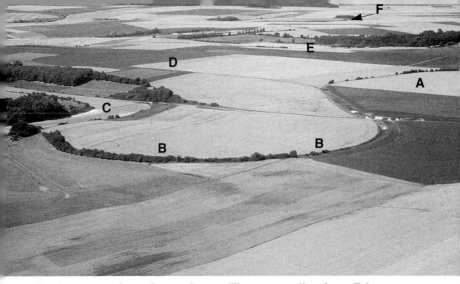

The Loop seen from the north-east. The pre-war line from Fricourt entered this upland area at A before describing the circle at B – B and dropping into the Vallée Raison at C on its way to Bray-sur-Somme. Loop Station on the British-built line from Dernancourt was at D; Happy Valley (Vallée du Bois Ricourt) was at E; Grovetown was at F. Regrettably, all the hedges and pathways marking the old railway lines have been ploughed up in recent years. (TP 1986)

the slope. Near the top, the road passed by a small excavated patch of land, now a scrubby pasture for cattle. This was Green Dump, a place for stores and ammunition, and (on this day) for tanks also. Having arrived in the early hours of 14 September, the tankmen spent the rest of the day here tuning their engines, checking their weapons and ammunition and taking on supplies. Rest was almost impossible, given

D Company's neighbours. The tanks of C Company in nearby Chimpanzee Valley. (Note their distinguishing ridged roofs of netting.)

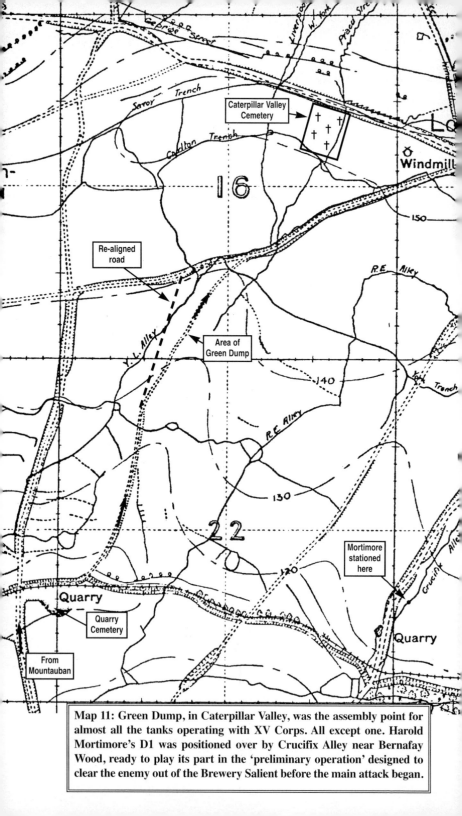

Map 11: Green Dump, in Caterpillar Valley, was the assembly point for almost all the tanks operating with XV Corps. All except one. Harold Mortimore's D1 was positioned over by Crucifix Alley near Bernafay Wood, ready to play its part in the 'preliminary operation' designed to clear the enemy out of the Brewery Salient before the main attack began.

Green Dump (marked with a cross) in Caterpillar Valley, the assembly point for the majority of tanks operating with XV Corps. Having left the Loop on the evening of 13 September, they climbed the road from the Quarry during the early hours and made Green Dump their temporary base. The following night they left for their battle positions. The photograph shows Longueval and Delville Wood on the right, with Flers and Gueudecourt behind them in the distance. On the left is High Wood. Caterpillar Valley Cemetery is in the middle of the photograph. (TP 1993)

the shattering roar of artillery all around them.

During the night of 14/15 September three of the four tanks allocated to 14th Division took the narrow road leading east from here up to the cross-roads just 400m west of Longueval, then entered the village by the main road. Beyond it they entered the wood, where Storey's tank D4 soon became ditched. Head and Blowers carried on as best they could to the northern rim.

At the same time the fourth tank, Mortimore's D1, had moved up from Bernafay Wood to its point of departure 100 yards south of the Longueval-Ginchy road, later leaving here at 5.15 a.m. to make history as the first tank in the world to engage in battle. He must have crossed the road roughly at its summit, a very slight rise only just discernible east of the present water-tower. Having shelled the edge of Delville Wood he then attacked the trenches of the Brewery – Hop, Beer and Ale – before being knocked out at a point which RFC photographs indicate was at map reference T13a 30.95. To reach this, go north out of Ginchy to the (post-War) civil cemetery, then turn left along the track beside it. At a point 620m from the cemetery a further track turns left (south) towards the edge of the wood where Ale Alley abutted it. But 90m short of this junction and 50m on your left is where D1 was hit. If you were to carry straight on, along the main track and past the junction (itself almost on top of the British eastern flank in James Street) you would arrive near the 'notch' of Delville Wood's northern rim. Cocoa Lane, where Head and Blowers set out, lay just 120m beyond it. Alternatively you can view this same spot by walking through the wood (where the South African Memorial is of course well worth a visit) to its northern perimeter fence.

From here, first Head then Blowers entered the shallow valley where No Man's Land lay, making for the German front line in Tea Support. To see this, take the next narrow track leading off the main road about 650m north of the Ginchy cemetery. Follow it to a point 100m beyond where the pylon cables pass above you. This is 40m from where the track at present ends and is where Cocoa Lane came down from the wood to your south. Tea Support lay 150m to the north, not quite on the highest ground but certainly on the skyline when viewed from below. It was somewhere near here that Head's D3 was hit but he eventually found shelter at the southern end of the *Rideau des Filoires*, the embankment topped with scrubby trees and a power pylon over on your left. The exact point was at its base, where an irrigation pool has recently been constructed. You will see this later, more clearly, from the Longueval-Flers road.

As for Blowers, he followed Cocoa Lane up to a point slightly left of the four trees on the horizon, where he arrived at the First Objective or Green Line. But he did not tarry. Crossing the Flers road just north of its highest point (spot height 151 on the I.G.N. map, the summit marked by those same four trees) he followed Gas Alley up to the Second Objective, or Brown Line, which lay along Gap Trench. To reach this, drive north to where the road takes a sharp left bend but also where a farm-track leads right. This point was the western end of Gap Trench, which led from here not by following the farm-track but rather by diverging increasingly from it towards the south. It crossed over Watling Street at a point 150m south of where the farm-track does. Alas, all trace of Watling Street south of here has been ploughed up, as has Fosse Way (*Chemin Vert du Moulin*), shown on the map as leading north from the bend on the Ginchy-Flers road. Both disappeared, most regrettably, as a result of the 1994-1995 *remembrement*. Both were features well known to British troops in this area in 1916.[iii]

If you are on foot, you can rejoin Blowers' path by walking east to Watling Street then northwards along its eastern rim until you reach Bulls Road. If in a car, drive into Flers itself then turn right at the memorial to the 41st Division, and down into a narrow lane. This was the start of Bulls Road, so called because it led over to the village of

Les Boeufs ('cattle' in French). It leads past Bulls Road Cemetery, then over a slight rise, just beyond which was the German battery which eventually destroyed Dolphin. The gun-pits were dug into the bank on your right which contemporary reports show was much deeper in 1916. The point finally reached by Blowers was in the middle of the field, also on your right, the exact trench-map reference being T1b 78.78. Just why the German gunners here failed to tackle Dolphin on its earlier northward approach along the side of Watling Street is a mystery. They certainly had a clear view of it but they may have been preoccupied with the British infantry immediately in front of them. Possibly, too, they left it to their comrades in the *Hohlwegzug* to deal with, although of course the guns here had been destroyed by their crews and the crews themselves killed or dispersed by British infantry just before Blowers first arrived on the scene.

Continuing down Bulls road, you come to Watling Street, where the unmade southern portion – not at all the 'shallow cutting' marked on the 1916 map – is still encased in the high banks which caused Blowers to remain on the rim above. But when he arrived at the junction he dropped down into Watling Street for his final advance. Follow this north for 500m to a pond and road junction (the road leading up and back to near the *Grabenzug* guns and to Point 91, of which more later) then for a further 100m to where Gird Trench lay. Shells were falling here – only a few heavies perhaps, but enough to persuade Blowers that to proceed further would be folly. The absence of infantry support must also have served to make him turn back. He was already 3kms from his start-point, his fuel was low and he still had to get back to Delville Wood. As we know, he did not reach it.

i. Strictly speaking, the Switch was that part of the trench which extended west from Point 93 on our maps but the name was applied loosely to parts further east. An attempt was later made to end the confusion by applying the name Tatler to the part facing 14th Division, and Serpentine to the part facing the Guards. However, the whole was still called the Flers Line on the map and since this name was equally shared with a trench further north some confusion must have remained.

ii Point 91 was the designation given by British troops to the German machine gun post here, being the last two digits of its nearest two-figure map reference, N32d 9.1. A four-figure reference would place it more accurately at N32d 92.12. Note that the map used here, issued five days before the battle, shows two German field guns east of Point 91, at N33c 15.05. They may have been the *Grabenzug* mentioned in the text but they are not visible on those air photographs which we have seen, whereas these do show two scorch marks in front of Gird Trench north of Point 91, at about N32d 8.4 and N32d 70.65. We have assumed, rightly or wrongly, that the guns were moved here at some stage prior to the battle.

iii *Remembrement* is a legal procedure in France designed to overcome the progressive fragmentation of land ownership to which France's system of small-holdings frequently gives rise. Every twenty, thirty or forty years all the land in a given agricultural area – extending over one, two or even three communes – is consolidated into larger units, the re-allocation to each farmer being made according to the extent and soil quality of his former holding. Unfortunately for the Great War historian and student, the process leads to old roads and tracks being destroyed and new ones laid down, the uprooting of hedgerows and embankments that feature on our trench-maps.

Chapter Four

15 SEPTEMBER
The New Zealand Divison

The New Zealand Division had arrived in France following the withdrawal from Gallipoli where, as part of the ANZAC contingent, its men had won much admiration for the courage and spirit they displayed during fighting on that accursed peninsula. Before coming to the Somme, they had been engaged in the Lys sector further north but a greater trial was yet to come. They were to be positioned between Flers and High Wood, their role being to safeguard the flank of XV Corps in its major thrust to the north.

But they had work to do before the battle began. At a conference held on 10 September Rawlinson had called for the potentially dangerous re-entrant which then existed in the British line north of

Men of 2/Auckland in a trench near Flers, 15 September. Taylor Library

Longueval to be filled up. By pushing forward the trenches here the attacking infantry would have less distance to cover before reaching the German front line, and their arrival there would be timed more or less to coincide with that of neighbouring units advancing on either side. The New Zealanders began the task by pushing forward saps from Tea Trench out into No Man's Land, and then – at least on the left if not on the right, where the German front line was already close – joining up their further ends into a continuous line. The results they named Auckland Trench and Otago Trench, after the battalions who had dug them, and Fern Trench after their national emblem.

The German front line now lay about 300-400 yards distant on the left, but only 200-300 yards distant on the right where the enemy still manned the sweeping bend of Coffee Lane. The First Objective, of course, was further on, by an average 200 yards or more, and lay along the mighty Switch Trench, hidden beyond the crest of the slope up which the New Zealanders had first to attack. Their divisional front was here 800-900 yards across, and was to remain so until they advanced beyond Flers, where it was eventually to narrow to nothing while

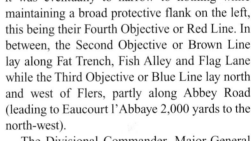

maintaining a broad protective flank on the left, this being their Fourth Objective or Red Line. In between, the Second Objective or Brown Line lay along Fat Trench, Fish Alley and Flag Lane while the Third Objective or Blue Line lay north and west of Flers, partly along Abbey Road (leading to Eaucourt l'Abbaye 2,000 yards to the north-west).

The Divisional Commander, Major-General Sir A.H. Russell, placed only two battalions in the front line – 2/Auckland on the right and 2/Otago on the left, both of 2 New Zealand Infantry Brigade. At 6.20 a.m. these men left their trenches, got into formation, then closed up behind the creeping barrage as it preceded them up the slope. As it moved, they could see the 'lanes' left in it for the tanks, but of the tanks themselves they could see nothing, for these were late in setting out from their start-point near Longueval, having been delayed by shell craters encountered during the night-time approach from Green Dump.

They were four in number. The first was D8,

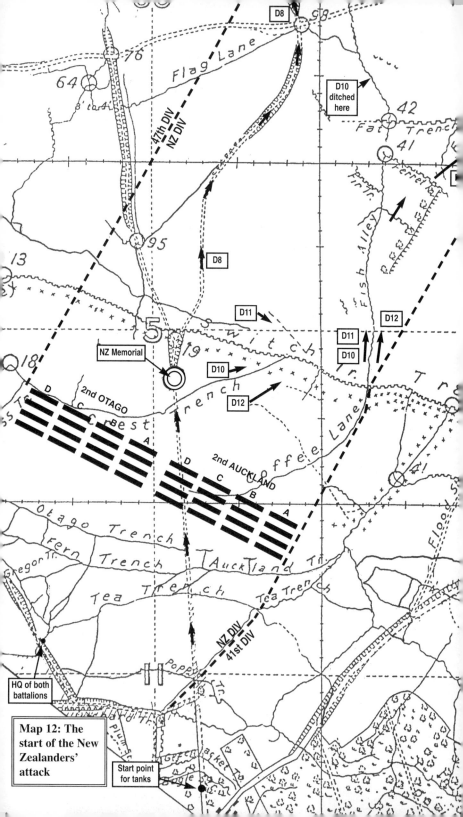

Map 12: The start of the New Zealanders' attack

commanded by Second Lieutenant H.G.F. Bown, leading the group up North Street towards the Fork. His task was to move along the extreme left flank of the divisional sector all the way up to its intended apex near Factory Corner, well north of Flers. He was to act alone, whereas the other three were to act in concert nearer to the village. This group consisted of D12 (Captain G. Nixon, the group's commander), D10 (Second Lieutenant H. Darby) and D11, Die Hard, (Second Lieutenant H.G. Pearsall).

Undeterred by the lack of support, the attacking infantry forced their way up the slope in fine style, singing. Little opposition was met in Coffee Lane but now withering fire came from the enemy in Crest Trench, and this caused severe casualties, although even here most of the opposition melted away in the face of the attackers' determined assault. On the left, however, a lone machine gun held up the Otago men until Sergeant Donald Brown and his comrade J. Rodgers crept forward, unobserved, then rose up to rush the enemy emplacement and kill the crew. The advance here then resumed. When they reached the First Objective, Brown and Rodgers again distinguished themselves by destroying a second machine gun and its crew. Brown himself repeated the exploit before the Second Objective was reached, and displayed great courage yet again in the later fighting between Flers and Eaucourt, where alas he was killed. He was awarded a posthumous VC. His grave is in the Warlencourt C.W.G.C. cemetery on the Albert-Bapaume road.

Sergeant Donald Brown.

The grave of Sergeant Donald Forrester Brown VC, in Warlencourt Military Cemetery.

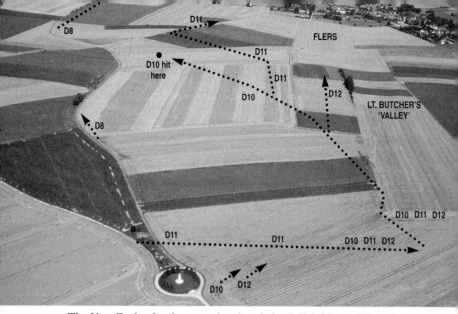

The New Zealanders' sector, showing their obelisk Memorial at the Fork and the routes taken by the four tanks supporting them. Note that the field pattern here, and indeed some of the roads, were modified during the *remembrement* of 1994-1995. The layout even of the Fork was changed after this picture was taken. (TP 1991)

The leading tank, Bown's D8, had been damaged on its way to the start line and the tail wheels were already useless, so he now had to make haste to catch up the leading waves of infantry. He was due to pause on Switch Trench and help 'mop up' any opposition there but this had largely been swamped by the speed of the advancing troops who by 6.50 a.m. had secured the Switch and begun to construct new trenches 60-100 yards beyond it. At 7.05 a.m. the attacking force – consisting now only of 4/Battalion of 3 New Zealand Rifle Brigade, spread out thinly across the whole divisional sector – was ready to move off again, fifteen minutes before their scheduled time. As soon as the creeping barrage resumed its forward progress and the infantry were able to move, Bown followed them, keeping to the right-hand branch of the Fork.

Meanwhile the other three had split, temporarily, Nixon and Darby turning along Crest Trench and Pearsall along Switch Trench, all three then joining up again and moving as a group up Fish Alley. It had originally been intended that Nixon should branch off to the right early on in order to clear the shallow valley lying east of the tree-lined embankment abutting Fig and Ferret trenches. This plan was apparently changed before the battle and now Nixon was heading west

60

of the trees, but it was here that he received a plea calling on him in effect to revert to his original task. A New Zealand officer wrote him a brief pencilled note saying:

> From Lieut. Butcher to O.C. 'Tanks'. Enemy machine guns appear to be holding up infantry in valley on your right. Can you assist in pushing forward? C.E. Butcher, Lieut. Commanding 15 Platoon, Reserve Company, 2/3 N.Z. (R.) B. 15/9/16, 9.15 a.m.

The message merits a place in history as the first written communication to a tank in action. It was carried through heavy gunfire by a New Zealand runner, Rifleman J.W. Dobson, who later wrote:

> The Germans had a pop at me once, and I got into a shell hole, and waited and then got going again. I got inside the tank and guided it to where these machine guns were, in a farm building, and the tank just pushed it over. Germans scattered in all directions.

While this was happening, Pearsall and Darby had moved up Fish Alley. It had been intended that when they arrived at the Second Objective (the junction of Fish Alley with Fat Trench) both tanks should bear right, join up again with Nixon and head round the westernmost edge of the village before making for the Third then the Fourth Objective in 41st Division's area between Gueudecourt and Factory Corner. But this part of the plan, like others, had been changed. Darby now continued northwards, alongside Fish Alley, his purpose being to come up behind the infantry held up by wire on the road leading into Flers from the direction of High Wood. These defences were part of the enemy's Flers Line (*Flers Riegel* or *Below Stellung*, named after General Fritz von Below), consisting of Flers Trench and Flers Support, which lay between the New Zealanders' Second and Third Objectives. It was not in itself an Objective or 'pause line' but was certainly very heavily wired and constituted a major obstacle, blocking the advance of the attacking infantry, now the Rifle Brigade's 2/Battalion on the right of the road and 3/Battalion on the left. The former were able to penetrate the wire in places but only with grievous loss. The latter were unable to move.

Darby drew closer to the road but at a point just north of Fat Trench the tank was hit by shell fire which shattered its prisms and temporarily blinded both the commander and driver. It was then hit by a second shell. One or other of these missiles smashed its track plates and caused other extensive damage, as a crew member, Gunner R. Frost, later explained:

An unidentified female tank moving over ground that looks fairly free of the marks of war, but then ground lying between the various barrage lines often did. Note also that it is photographed from low down, from what appears in the bottom right-hand corner to be a shell-hole or trench in which the photographer – apparently a soldier advancing with the tanks – was perhaps sheltering. On the (admittedly slender) evidence here we believe the photograph must have been taken during the course of the battle, rather than 'staged' at some point thereafter.

A female Mark I, ditched. Again we cannot identify the machine for sure but Darby's D10 could well have looked like this after its encounter with German 77mm shellfire at Fish Alley. After all, some reports actually said it had fallen into the trench (by attempting to cross it at too oblique an angle) rather than being hit by shells. But perhaps both accounts are true; D10 could have tipped into the trench when it was made 'uncontrollable' as described by Gunner Frost. So could the tank shown here be the same as that shown in the preceding photograph? They are certainly placed next to each other in the private album from which these shots have been copied. Moreover, both photographs show similar camouflage markings, both show similar gear stowed on the roof, and both show an ammunition box on the tail assembly. Individually these items may not be conclusive but together they argue for both tanks being one and the same. And since they are coupled in the album with other photographs of New Zealand troops we think the case for identifying this tank as Darby's is strong. (Both photographs by courtesy of Geoff Bridger.)

Another tank, also taken from the 'New Zealand' album of private photographs. If this was indeed one of those operating with the New Zealand Division on 15 September it can only be Nixon's D12, a male, which ended up at Fort Trench. It shows no outward sign of the fire which followed its ditching, but this was found to be the case with at least one other tank left burning on the battlefield. Courtesy of Geoff Bridger

> *It didn't come through the tank, but it buckled the plating and on the inside of that plate all the controls were mounted on cast-iron brackets. Well, the cast-iron didn't buckle but it broke. All the controls fell on the floor, so the tank was completely uncontrollable. You couldn't do anything with it.*

Together with his crew, Darby, partly blinded by splinters of glass from the visor prisms, abandoned the tank and joined the infantry in Fish Alley.

Seeing what had happened to D10 and realising that the infantry further forward were still held up, Pearsall in D11 decided to swing away from his own course and carry out the task which Darby had been unable to finish. He approached the German wire, flattened it with the weight of Die Hard's 27 tons, and allowed the New Zealanders to pass across, in the process capturing a hundred prisoners. This was exactly what the inventors and advocates of the tank had foreseen as its principal role – destroying those obstacles which stood in the infantry's way.

Having crossed this major barrier, the New Zealanders on the left advanced onto Abbey Road and into the fields to its north. They were now on the Third Objective. Their comrades on the right were less fortunate in so far as they had spilled over into the neighbouring sector in order to clear the houses in Flers which 41st Division had not so far reached, and this had delayed their progress. Another setback there was

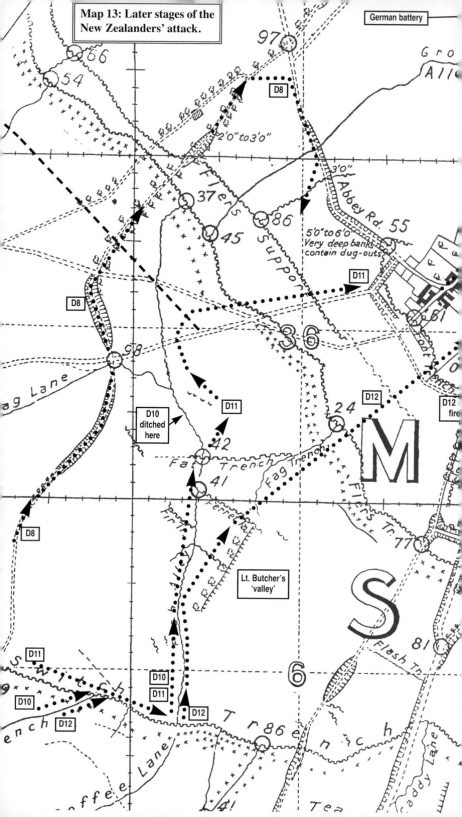

Map 13: Later stages of the
New Zealanders' attack.

German battery

the loss of Nixon's tank D12. It had gone forward along the west side of the village but had there been hit by shell fire which damaged its steering. Nixon withdrew his machine but it then fell into a shell hole and became ditched. While it was being dug out a second shell hit it and set it on fire. The crews of the tanks serving with 41st Division ran across to help put out the blaze but to no avail. One crew member, Gunner William Debenham, perished in the incident.

Despite this loss, the New Zealanders here eventually pushed on northwards, only to find themselves confronted by a pocket of resistance led by one *Leutnant* Braunhofer in the fields west of the Ligny road. Evidently aided by Pearsall's D11, as well as by the men of 41st Division and their tanks, they finally overran the position and took the defenders prisoner. Once this task was completed, they pushed further up the Ligny road to a point beyond its junction with Glebe Street. Here, however, they were much exposed to enemy fire from places ahead and on either flank and were forced to withdraw.

The New Zealand Rifle Brigade's 1/Battalion had now come up to

The fields north-west of Flers where *Leutnant* Braunhofer attempted a final stand against the men of 41st and New Zealand Divisions. (TP 1986)

relieve 2/ and 3/Battalions in order to carry the attack forward and seize the Fourth Objective. Setting out from Abbey Road at 11.30 a.m., they advanced across the fields north of Flers and mounted a spirited assault on Grove Alley (*Kronprinz Weg*) where some German field guns and their crews were captured. But again the area was found to be too exposed to machine gun fire from the north and west and the New Zealanders were obliged to fall back. As they did so, German reserve troops bombed their way back up the trench and recaptured the guns.

In the afternoon there were a number of reports indicating the imminence of German counterattacks against Flers and the action of 41st Division's tanks in repelling these will be discussed in the next chapter. But what of the two machines still working with the New Zealanders?

One of these, Bown's D8, had done valuable work along the extreme west flank of the divisional sector, for the area beyond here was still occupied by Germans left in possession of ground which 47th (2nd London) Division had been unable to reach, weakened as they were by the severity of the struggle in High Wood. Bown had certainly served to keep the enemy's heads down and thus reduce the danger to the New Zealanders around him, but he may also have helped reduce the risks facing the battered 47th. He had paid a price for this, for he too, like Darby, was temporarily blinded by glass from his shattered visor prism. His driver, Private B.J. Young, was in the same condition.

We do not know when D8 arrived at the Third Objective on Abbey Road but it is possible that it was around the time that 1/Battalion were withdrawing from Grove Alley. Bown no doubt decided that, given his

New Zealand's Memorial to the Missing, in Caterpillar Valley Cemetery, Longueval.

and his driver's inability to see properly, he was ill fitted to help the attack forward. We have to remember too that like all the tank commanders he had been given strict instructions not to let his machine fall into enemy hands – a hazard which in the circumstances was not to be ruled out.

In any case, XV Corps issued an order at 2.50 p.m. calling on all units to consolidate on the Third Objective, the Blue Line. A further order at 3.30 p.m. said there would be no fresh attacks until the following day; meanwhile, all tanks still operational were to return to base and prepare for action on the morrow. Bown accordingly headed back south.

The other tank commander, Pearsall, was still in the area but he seems not to have received the order to withdraw. Or, more probably, he received it but chose to ignore it in the light of a New Zealand request that he should stand ready to resist any German counter-attack launched against their flank. We know that Pearsall agreed to this, for at one stage the R.F.C. reported him out on the road north of the village. We do not know precisely when this was although he certainly remained out until at least 7.45 p.m., and even then merely pulled back into the village rather than back to base.

We do know, however, that his efforts had been much valued by the New Zealanders, especially for his help in a further bout of fighting during the afternoon. One of their officers later reported:

> As the infantry dug in, they were covered by the tank, His Majesty's Landship Die Hard, commanded by a gallant young officer of the Highland Light Infantry. It had already done strenuous service, though none of its adventures so impressed its cheerful crew as the sight of passing Bavarians hurriedly adjusting their respirators, under the impression that the smoke from the exhaust pipe was some novel kind of lethal gas. It now moved along the road towards Factory Corner, protecting the digging parties with its broadsides and at the same time firing up the road with its forward guns.

The New Zealanders' identification of this officer as a member of the HLI is an error. Pearsall, whose tank Die Hard was the only one left in the area and is the man clearly intended, was formerly in the Royal Artillery. The HLI officer, Stuart Hastie, commander of Dinnaken, had returned to the rear during the morning, as we shall see in the next chapter.

There is a footnote to Pearsall's service with the New Zealanders. Two footnotes in fact. The first concerns the reported sighting by the

RFC of a tank *in action* at N26a 0.3, well forward in ground still held by the Germans, only 350 yards south of the Gueudecourt-Factory Corner road and just 150 yards from the Gird Line. The time was 1.30 p.m. The likelihood is that this was an error by the aircraft's observer, misled by the shadows in the shell holes which here abounded, but if it was not, then the tank was most probably Pearsall's.[i]

The second incident is more bizarre. An RFC observer reported that between 6.25 and 6.45 p.m. a tank was in action at N26d 8.7, in fields south-east of Gueudecourt. This was a long way from the New Zealand sector and a most unlikely place for any tank to be. General Rawlinson thought so too, and ordered a new reconnaissance. This was duly repeated and the sighting was confirmed. Indeed, several other aircraft were said to have backed up the report. Again, there is no other evidence to support this, but if the report was true, then the tank can only have been Pearsall's Die Hard, for all other tanks can be accounted for.

Could he *really* have reached this far?

Gueudecourt and (in the distance) Flers, seen from the north-east. A point in the middle of the fields in the lower left portion of this photograph is where the RFC reported seeing a tank in action during the evening of 15 September. The only candidate is Pearsall's D11, Die Hard, but can he really have travelled this far? (TP 1986)

Field Guide

We have already seen Green Dump, where the tanks were stationed during the day of 14 September, and have followed their route into Longueval. Their start point was where the main road leading out towards Flers formed a junction with the minor road – known as North Street to the British – which led up to the Fork, situated a few metres beyond where the New Zealand memorial now stands. The New Zealand front line lay 400m past the Crucifix, while the German front line in Coffee Lane was on the right another 150m further up. Crest Trench crossed North Street just short of the road surrounding the monument and it was here that Nixon and Darby turned right. Switch Trench, where Pearsall also turned right to rejoin these other two, was just over the crest beyond the monument but, before going on, the visitor should spend a few minutes here to reflect on the bravery and self-sacrifice of men who came 'from the uttermost ends of the earth' to fight and die in the fields around you. In these very fields.

The left-hand branch of the Fork has unfortunately been re-aligned recently but the right-hand track used by Bown *(Chemin de Justice)* is still intact, so drive down here for 1km to the junction with the track leading from High Wood towards Flers. The continuation beyond this junction has recently been ploughed up and other tracks nearby have been re-aligned, so you may not be able to follow this part of Bown's route too closely. Instead, follow the road leading right. At a point just 150m from the junction and 120m into the fields on the right was where Darby ditched in Fish Alley. At a point 400m from the junction lay the Flers Line, where Pearsall came to crush the wire and let the infantry through.

The New Zealand Memorial at the Fork. It commemorates men who came 'from the uttermost ends of the earth' to die in the fields around it.

Continue on to Abbey Road. Still blinded by the glass, Bown came in here from the left before turning for home. Pearsall, too, may have taken this route to reach the village and the Ligny road leading to the north. In 1916 the embankments of Abbey Road, deeper perhaps than today, were lined with German dugouts. Today they seem to be a repository for unexploded ordnance recovered from the fields, so beware! The place where Pearsall stood guard with the New Zealanders during the late afternoon was probably the junction of the main road with Glebe Street, a track (now disappeared) leading off to the right 300m north of the village.

To see the two places, much further forward, where the RFC reported having seen a tank or tanks in action, drive north to Factory Corner then turn right and right again to Grass Lane A.I.F. Burial Ground. Standing by its south-eastern corner, N26a 0.3 lies 100m to the east. *If* the sighting was accurately reported the tank could, just, have been Pearsall's Die Hard. Now drive into Gueudecourt and down *Rue des Guilmonniers*. A couple of hundred metres on, a field appears on the left. It was in the middle of this field, at N26d 8.7, that the RFC reported seeing a tank in action during the evening. In this instance, Pearsall's Die Hard was the only possible candidate, however unlikely it may seem that he could have reached so far.

Let us not forget Nixon's D12. A narrow passage runs west from the main street of Flers to the fields behind. Here turn left for just 70m and you are standing where his tank caught fire and where Gunner Debenham died.

---

[i] It has to be said that a later map shows a wrecked tank near the spot but this could, just, date from later fighting. More probably it is a cartographic error, for the location given is 330 yards NNW from the wreck of D14 at N26c 30.75 (see Chapter 6). Significantly, the same map gives an erroneous location for the wreck of D5 which is also 330 yards NNW from the actual place.

Chapter Five

15 SEPTEMBER
41st Division

As we have seen, the British Army's main effort on this day was to be made in the area of XV Corps. Of the ten divisions employed along the whole front, 41st Division and 14th Division had the task of carrying the attack furthest forward, penetrating 4000 yards (3650m) into German-held territory, but the 41st in particular was faced with the formidable defence-works around Flers as well as the Gird Line protecting Gueudecourt.

The division had three brigades to throw into the attack. On the right, with a frontage from Cocoa Lane to the Longueval-Flers road, was 124 Brigade. On the left of the road was 122 Brigade, while 123 Brigade was held in reserve. The front line ran 300-400 yards north of Delville Wood, through whose shattered trees the communication trenches brought up hundreds, thousands of men during the night of 14/15 September to await Zero at 6.20 a.m.

The attack was to be supported by ten tanks. Their crews, already tired by weeks of training, maintenance tasks, driving, demonstrations, and preparations for battle, had left the Loop on the evening of 13 September and spent the following day at Green Dump. When darkness fell, they began the wearisome journey up to their departure points a mile away, north of Longueval on the Flers road. One officer, Lieutenant A.E. Arnold, who perhaps understandably remembered the distance as being very much longer, later wrote:

I have always been puzzled as to why it took nine hours – from 9.00 p.m. to 6.00 a.m. – to traverse that distance, for we seemed to be travelling the whole time, and certainly made no deliberate stops. But it was a case of bottom gear all the time, and on good ground bottom gear only produced a 'speed' of about 1,000 yards per hour. But it was necessary at times for one of the crew to get out and scout a way round a particularly bad patch. Evidently, with the occasional stops and much laborious climbing out of shell craters, we could only have maintained a rate of travel of six or seven hundred yards an hour, and shortly after midnight it became clear that it was a race against time, despite what seemed a sufficiently early start.

122 Brigade reported to 41st Division H.Q. that the tanks were safely in position by 3.20 a.m. but this was not Arnold's recollection.

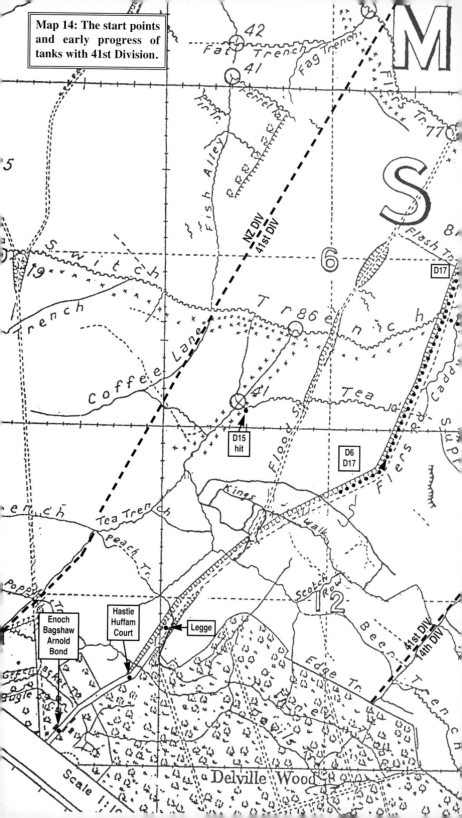

Map 14: The start points and early progress of tanks with 41st Division.

As the dawn began to show the ground up, we were still so far behind the front that it seemed certain we could not get there by Zero hour, for the 'going' was now simply one succession of shell craters. But the ground was dry and it was thrilling, the way the tank would go down into a crater, stick the upstanding parts of her tracks into the opposite wall and then climb steadily out. The rate of progress was now desperately slow, and I suppose the last thousand yards took two hours to cover. The night had passed like a flash, and I felt for a while a sense of despair: it seemed so impossible that we could arrive in time to be of any use to the infantry. In fact, I thought of sending off a pigeon with a message to say we were behind the hunt. But I reflected that such a message would be useless to anyone and did not send it. Fortunately so, for we were getting nearer to the front line than I thought, and although the infantry were out of the trenches before we arrived, we now made better time, for No Man's Land had not been so heavily shelled and the going was better.

The tanks were divided into four groups, C, D, E and F, all their start-points being on or adjacent to the lower stretch of the Flers road north-west of Delville Wood. In front, leading the attack as the sole member of Group C, was Second Lieutenant R.C. Legge in D6. Behind him came Group D, consisting of Lieutenant S.H. Hastie in D17 (Dinnaken), Second Lieutenant V. Huffam in D9 (Dolly), and Second Lieutenant G.F. Court in D14. Behind these, Groups E and F

The start-point of the tanks with 41st Division and New Zealand Division, just outside Longueval. A = Legge; B = Hastie, Huffam and Court; C = Bagshaw, Arnold, Bond and Enoch; D = Bown, Darby, Pearsall and Nixon. (T.P. 1991)

assembled near the junction with North Street. The first of these was to include Captain S.S. Sellick in D19, Lieutenant H.R. Bell in D2 and Lieutenant J.L. Bagshaw in D15. F Group included Lieutenant A.E. Arnold in D16 (Dracula), Lieutenant A.J. Enoch in D7 and Second Lieutenant L.C. Bond in D18.

Not all of these tanks went into battle. Sellick and Bell ditched in shell holes on the way up. Enoch started out but ditched early in the passage across No Man's Land. Huffam and Court both crashed into a disused dugout at the outset and according to Huffam needed help from a Chinese labour unit to extricate themselves, by which time they were too late to take part.

It had earlier been ordered that Group D should move along the east side of Flers, while Group E would go through the village itself and Group F would move up its western side. However, this plan was amended shortly before the battle, possibly because of casualties on the way up or because of a changed perception of where the main enemy opposition would be. It was now decreed that Group D would go through the village and Group E would join Group F on its west side. Legge in Group C would stay east of the village, but now closer to it than his original orders had said, and as far as possible carry out on his own all that the three tanks of group D had been expected to do.

As the tanks assembled, the infantry up ahead of them waited in the darkness, finding what shelter they could in the battered trenches. Those on the right of the Flers road were from 124 Brigade, the front battalions being 10/Queen's (Royal West Surrey) and 21/KRRC. Behind them were 32/ and 26/Royal Fusiliers. West of the road were

The original caption of this photograph says 'Tanks ditched at Longueval on their first day out. Dug out by 4/South Lancashire, 15/9/16. Shell bursting on left.' The machines in question are undoubtedly those of Huffam and Court, although Huffam went on record later as saying that the tanks were dug out by men of a Chinese labour unit. Both accounts could be true; Chinese labourers were possibly attached to the Lancashire pioneers for this task.
(Courtesy of the Museum of the Queen's Lancashire Regiment, and with thanks to Bob Grundy.)

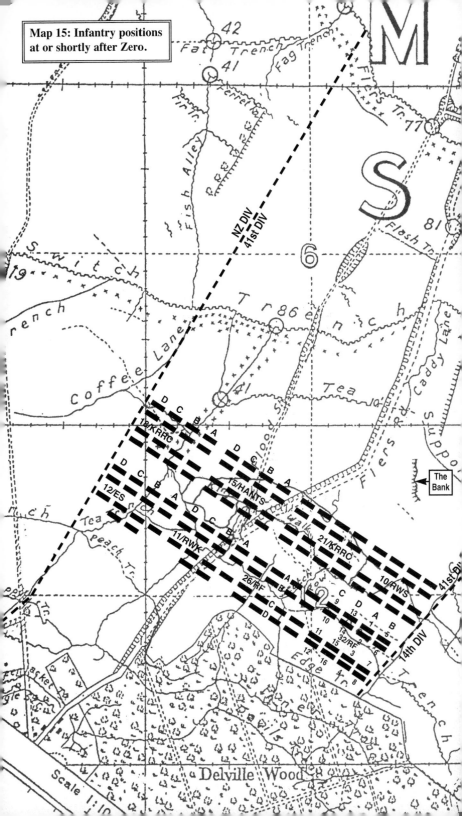

Map 15: Infantry positions at or shortly after Zero.

Soldiers moving up to the front line on a congested road near Fricourt.

men of 122 Bde, with 15/Hampshire and 18/KRRC in front, followed by 11/Royal West Kent and 12/East Surrey. A few days before, most of these men had been living in the peaceful villages of the lower Somme – training for the battle ahead, certainly, but still enjoying life in rural tranquillity. Then they began their long journey up to the line, first by train, then on foot over ground increasingly torn and shattered by war – Bécordel, Fricourt, Mametz, Montauban and Caterpillar Valley. On the way they had passed weary, stricken men marching raggedly in the opposite direction, men gaunt with fatigue, ashen in face and with haggard eyes, men who had witnessed violence and death at very close quarters. Now their replacements were making the final approach.

Presently we dropped into a communication trench and then began that laborious serpentine crawl that seemed to have no end. At first it was not so bad; the companies behind kept touch and progress was steady, if slow. But messages began to pass along the line, from front to rear, from rear to front. We would come to a halt. 'Pass the word back to close up.' The message would fade away to silence along the line, and then there would be a seemingly interminable delay until the reply would come

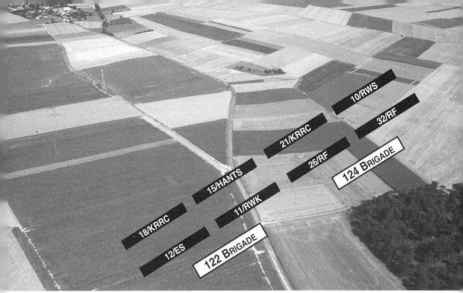

41st Division deployed for battle north of Delville Wood. Diagrammatic only. (TP 1991)

from the rear. We would stagger forward again... just like a concertina opening and closing... .Dimly we realised from the shattered stumps that we were in Delville Wood and those gifted with a sense of smell experienced the stench of that horrible place... .We encountered dead bodies at more frequent intervals, gruesome stinking shapes. The Colonel with his torch identified on some the black buttons of the Rifles [KRRC]. Oh! that dreadful night during which we crawled like snails through the midst of horrors less darkly imagined than actually realised. Well was it called Devil's Wood.

So wrote Sergeant Norman Carmichael of 21/KRRC, whose C Company was to be in the first wave of the attacking force, facing the Germans in Tea Support Trench which here ran along the top of a prominent embankment.

We found ourselves in what we supposed was the front line trench... Our platoon clambered over the parapet; one or two shook hands rather awkwardly with pals left behind, and we went forward into No Man's Land where we lay down to wait for Zero... .We could just discern the dim outline of the bank in front, on the top of which was the German trench, [and] the silhouettes of German tin hats moving about. Our opponents were apparently becoming anxious, as well they might, for I am sure that they could not miss seeing, through the gloom, something of the movement in our lines.

77

This may well have alerted the Germans, who sent over a number of shells from time to time, as if searching for troop concentrations. One particularly unfortunate shot, landing just before Zero, killed the Commanding Officer of 18/KRRC (Lieutenant-Colonel C.P. Marten), his Adjutant, his Signalling Officer and his Trench Mortar Officer.

The secret of the tank had been well kept and, to begin with, had been restricted to senior officers in each battalion. Later this was relaxed and all officers were told. But by Zero on 15 September most men in the trenches knew that a new weapon of war was going to be used, and some had even witnessed its progress up to the front. Others now sensed its arrival in the gloom around them, heard the quiet throb of its motor 'idling' as it waited, or made out its approaching shape in the lightening dawn. Eventually individual machines could be distinguished and men watched in wonderment as they clanked and ground their way ahead.

For the men waiting on either side of the road the minutes seemed to drag. Those further forward were at first denied the reassurance provided by the presence of the tanks, which were late in coming up; at 6.20 a.m. the leading tank, Legge's D6, was only part way through the British front trenches. Then at last, says Carmichael,

> *...a great flash lit up the whole of the sky behind us, and we*

The attack on Flers, seen from above Delville Wood. With Bagshaw out of action, Bond and Arnold pressed on, alongside Flood Street (until recently a chalk track, *le Chemin Blanc*, now asphalted). Meanwhile, Hastie approached Flers along the main road and Legge began his swing to the east, avoiding the steep embankments of Flers Avenue. Thereafter he returned to give valuable support to the infantry on the east side of the village. (TP 1991)

heard a tremendous rumbling roar, followed by the sound of the coming shells, like that of an on-coming express train, culminating in a piercing shriek overhead. Then the ground in front of us seemed to heave up in a lurid burst of yellow flame, and we were on the brink of an inferno of crashing explosions. Surely there could not be a German left alive in that trench of theirs!

In the dark before dawn the leading British ranks on the left of the road, 15/Hampshire and 18/KRRC, who were both only 200 yards from the enemy, had withdrawn a short distance so as to reduce the chance of 'shorts' in the British barrage causing casualties, but when the guns opened up at Zero they surged forward again, formed up behind the barrage and then followed it forward as it began its awesome progress.

Here as elsewhere some had been allotted the task of removing wounded from the path of the tanks and the work soon became necessary as men in the first waves fell to machine guns and shrapnel. Those first few minutes saw hideous losses. In 11/RWK alone three company commanders and the greater proportion of their officers were early casualties. So too were the senior NCOs, out in front leading their men on.

In Sergeant Carmichael's No.10 Platoon, in C Company of 21/KRRC – the Yeoman Rifles, from Yorkshire – disaster quickly struck even as he watched one of his section commanders advancing.

I kept an anxious eye on Kidd's section and, sure enough, before they had gone very far, one of those confounded shells landed right in their midst, blowing them down like ninepins. I distinctly saw poor Kidd throw up his arms, and then I knew that that lovable, generous soul, whom I had known since the very beginning at Helmsley, had 'gone west'. There were only two or three survivors in the section, and those very gallant fellows dragged the bodies of their killed and wounded comrades out of the path of the oncoming tank, and then went on.

Then Carmichael was wounded, shot through the leg, before he had even reached the first German trench, Tea Support.

I rolled over into a shell hole. Lance Corporal Mitchell, commander of No. 7 section and a great favourite of mine, bent over me and inquired 'Are you alright, Sergeant?' I replied 'I'm alright. Go on.' No sooner were the words out of my mouth than a shrapnel shell burst ten feet over our heads. The splendid chap settled forward on his face, and there he knelt with a hole right through his head... .

79

What was left of the platoon was still moving slowly but steadily forward and the succeeding waves were passing me. I saw their well-known faces, wide-eyed and drawn, but all pushing steadily on... . .In front I could make out two or three of No.7 section – Jim Hutchinson I knew was one – climbing up the bank into the trench. Another figure a little to their right had almost reached the top when a shell burst right in his back... .The barrage had moved forward by now. The second company was coming past in little knots of men, looking fearfully at the mangled bodies of dead and wounded that littered this death-stricken ground. ...In the shell holes round about me I could see arms waving and hear the pitiful cries of the wounded shouting for assistance. Still bodies in strange unnatural attitudes lay dotted about here and there.

Carmichael had earlier seen a tank 'lumbering past on my left, belching forth yellow flame from her Vickers gun, and making for the gap where the Flers road cut through the enemy trench'. This must have been Legge's D6, which rounded the main bend of the Flers road at 6.45 a.m., or perhaps Hastie in D17 following on behind (although, being 'males', both had Hotchkiss 6-pounders rather than Vickers machine guns). Having crossed the German front line, Legge then had to approach the Switch – the First Objective – where he was to leave the road and turn right. After just 150 yards, he then bore to the left, hoping to follow Gate Lane as in his instructions, but this trench was badly 'knocked about' and must have been unrecognisable as a trench, which would explain why he was spotted by the RFC some distance from it, at T1c 6.5, struggling through the shell-torn wilderness.

West of the Flers road the German front line in Tea Support had been virtually obliterated but the German guns beyond it were still at work and Bagshaw's D15 became the next casualty even as he reached it. The commander and his crew abandoned the burning tank but two of the men were then shot and killed and others were wounded. Now the sole survivors of Groups E and F – Arnold and Bond – moved steadily on. Meanwhile Hastie, on their right, could be seen on the main road approaching the broad bands of wire protecting Flers, in front of which lay the British infantry, already sadly depleted in numbers but now pinned down and helpless. Any attempt by them to move forward meant certain death. But then Hastie came up, crushed the wire, placed his tank astride the Flers Line where it crossed the road in front of the village and enfiladed the occupants. Resistance collapsed.

Map 16: Later routes of tanks with 41st Division.

The southern entrance to Flers. The Germans' main trench defending the village lay just short of the junction with the road back to Ginchy. Hastie crossed the wire and the trench itself with the greatest ease. (TP 1986)

The way into Flers was now open. Hastie took Dinnaken up the road to the point where it bent round to the right, then left past the ruins of the church. With his crew firing at German strong points with their 6-pounder guns, he then moved down the straight stretch in the village proper with parties of infantry following. Above, the crew of an RFC aircraft watched the scene enacted, then headed back to the British lines to deliver that famous message: 'A tank is walking up the High

Hastie's tank D17, Dinnaken, 'walking up the High Street of Flers with the British Army cheering behind', from a drawing in the Daily Mirror. The church is on the wrong side of the road, but that is a mere detail! A tank in action was what the British public needed to see. (Daily Mirror 1916)

Flers High Street, before the battle, looking south from La Place.

Street of Flers with the British army cheering behind'. These words, or various versions of them, were then repeated around the world by journalists happy to have at least some encouraging news to report from the bloodbath of the Somme.

The infantry now in Flers included remnants of various battalions – one hundred from 18/KRRC under Captain R. Baskett, men of 11/RWK under Second Lieutenant P.T. Cooksey, a party of 8/East Surrey under Lieutenant W. Staddon and a group of 15/Hampshire – in all, 300 men of 122 Brigade. There was a contingent also from 124 Brigade including a party of officers and men from 32/Royal Fusiliers. And the New Zealanders poured over from their own sector on the west to help clear out German dugouts threatening their flank.

Flers High Street, before the battle. A German photograph looking north from the church tower. From *An der Somme*.

The ruins of Flers. Taylor Library

All, however, were suddenly confronted by danger when a German bombardment of the village came crashing down. There was a speedy move to reach cover, to shelter from the storm of high explosive now unleashed, and many of the men filtered back to the trenches south of the village. Regrettably command, control and cohesion were lost and the tendency within the village to withdraw spread across to the rest of 124 Brigade on its eastern edge, Lieutenant-Colonel Oakley of 10/Queens thinking that he had to conform. The position needed to be restored, but it was not until later in the day that the Brigade Major of 122 Brigade, Major Gwyn Gwyn-Thomas, came up from the rear to organise a force of officers and men to go forward north of the village to re-establish a viable defence there. He was probably surprised to discover, on arrival, that the garrison had never abandoned the place. Not only were officers and men of 122 Brigade present in various parts of northern Flers but the New Zealanders were in possession of Box and Cox trenches – and the tanks were nearby as well!

Meanwhile, what of Hastie? Well, he eventually reached the tiny square near the north end of the village before realising that the supporting infantry were no longer with him. They were either sheltering from the bombardment or were retreating to the trenches

south of the village. Hastie, also, was worried about this bombardment – he was acutely aware that Dinnaken was not shell-proof – so he too withdrew, his intentions reinforced by realisation that his engine was not in a fit state to continue for much longer. He retraced his path past the ruined church and then back

Stuart Hastie, wearing the M.C. awarded to him for his action on this day. He is also now wearing the uniform of the Machine Gun Corps rather than that of the Highland Light Infantry, his original regiment.

La Place, today La Place des Britanniques, where Hastie turned round. It is now the site of a monument to men of 41st Division. (TP 1986)

The Bank or *Rideau des Filoires*, between Longueval and Flers. Hastie's D17 came to rest at the north (left-hand) end, Head's D3 at the south (right-hand) end. (TP 1986)

to the Flers Line, crowded with troops leaderless and confused owing to casualties among officers and NCOs. Continuing south, he eventually came to the main bend in the road where he decided that the tank could go no further. Before the engine died entirely he coaxed it across to the nearby bank, hoping to find there some shelter for both men and machine.

D17, Dinnaken, at the *Rideau des Filoires*, in later use as a brigade headquarters. (IWM)

He was watched by Sergeant Carmichael, who had sought similar refuge, together with other wounded. From his vantage point by the bank he had witnessed the whole vast spectacle of an army on the attack – its advancing battalions, its dead and its dying, the enemy's angry response, the shelling and the fury and the screams and the noise. At one point he looked back to see a team of pioneers starting to repair shell holes on the crest of the road leading up from Longueval, where the British front trenches had crossed it. The Germans must have spotted them, for they began bombarding them, apparently with heavy shells. Casualties occurred, light at first and then more seriously, one salvo landing in their midst. The survivors wavered, then scattered as more shells landed.

And now the stage was set for as thrilling a sight as I ever witnessed in the war. On the crest of the ridge appeared a team of cantering horses, dragging the first gun, followed at regular intervals by the others. The enemy was now fully alive as to what was going on, and redoubled his shelling. Still the leading gun drew rapidly nearer, seeming to be miraculously immune. But it was on the crossing of the trench that the Boche had concentrated his barrage of grey-bursting H.E. mixed with shrapnel. When they came to where the road mending had finished, the horses were put to a gallop and the gun and limber bumped and tossed over the shell holes. Once or twice it appeared as if the force of an explosion had blown the whole lot over, but by some miracle the gun wheeled round beside us in the shelter of the bank – that is shelter from H.E. but not from shrapnel. The other guns were not all so fortunate. One had its limber hit, but somehow the gun was brought on. The four pieces were pushed round, the limbers unloaded of their shells, and the horses spurred to a hell-for-leather gallop back through the barrage up the road to Longueval. As one of the teams was just starting off, a shrapnel burst a few feet overhead. The front four horses fell, and the remaining driver reeled in his saddle and came tumbling to the ground. To our surprise he scrambled to his feet, unhitched his two horses, remounted, and went tearing off towards safety. Then the ammunition limbers began to arrive with their loads of shells. They suffered more than the guns had done. One team was knocked completely out of action at that fateful corner and the wreckage had to be rounded by those following. But wonderfully the guns were supplied with their stacks of shells and the empty limbers were off again, bouncing

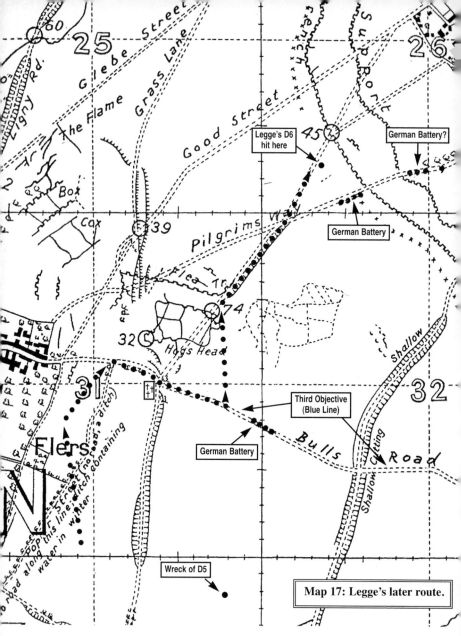

Map 17: Legge's later route.

Labels on map: Ligny Rd, Glebe Street, The Flame, Grass Lane, Good Street, Support, French, German Battery?, Legge's D6 hit here, German Battery, Pilgrims Wa..., Tea Tr., Box, Cox, Hog's Head, Flers, Shallow, Shallow Cutting, Bulls Road, Third Objective (Blue Line), German Battery, Wreck of D5, r road along this line (no road, a ditch) S...r Street (no road, a ditch) water in winter containing

about like mad things, with artillery men clinging like limpets to their precarious perches. ...Later on in the war I have seen field artillery going into action in the open, and in much greater numbers, but never have I been so thrilled as I was on that memorable afternoon in front of Delville wood.

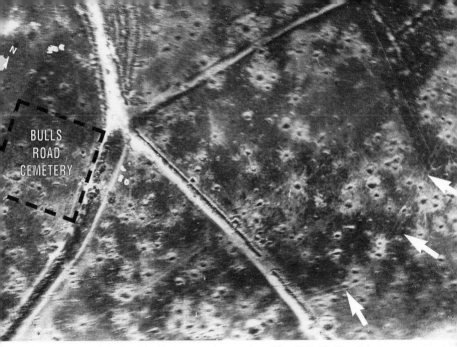

The track marks of Legge's D6 as he turned north off Bulls Road just short of the crest, having – so he must have thought – neutralised the German battery lying a short distance away (off the photograph, bottom right). Note the tracks south of Bulls Road. They could be the marks made by Legge's approach but they appear to be slightly narrower than those of a tank (possibly the path made earlier by a gun of the German battery?), so we incline to the view that Legge approached from the lower, hidden ground off to the top of the picture. Had he approached over the open ground from the south he would surely have been blown to pieces, for the guns here had just destroyed Blowers' D5 at a much greater range. Note also the blurred image in this photograph which was taken on 17 September when the weather was poor. The pilot had to fly very low to avoid heavy clouds, thus increasing the apparent speed of the aircraft. (Enlargement of a part of 3c 959 in the IWM)

Clearly the order to the artillery to get forward as soon as they possibly could had been complied with here if not elsewhere. One man who would have been glad of this was Legge, now well ahead on the east side of Flers. He had done much good work here, as the commanding officer of 26/Royal Fusiliers later testified:

> *This tank was of the greatest material use and the party in charge of it distinguished themselves considerably.*

Legge set off again, this time for his assault on the Third Objective (the Blue Line) which ran along Bulls Road. But he was now alone, for the infantry of 124 Bde which was supposed to attack at the same time was nowhere to be seen. Legge would of course have been looking through his visor at the ground ahead, not to the rear. Had this not been so he might have seen the infantry drifting back to the Flers Line, away from the battle, following their commander's orders issued when the neighbouring 122 Bde was found to be falling back under bombardment.

So he continued north, using dead ground by the ditch shown on his map, thus following the route originally planned for the three tanks of Group D. Also shown on his map was the German battery on Bulls Road, just ahead of him. And to his right was the still burning wreck of D5, Dolphin, Blowers' tank knocked out by that same battery no more than thirty minutes before.

So Legge undoubtedly knew the enemy guns were there. Undoubtedly, too, he took the decision to destroy them for he spurned the easy, direct route to his next Objective near Gueudecourt and instead changed direction right, mounted Bulls Road and followed it to a point just short of the crest but within sight of the battery 100 yards away. Precisely what happened here we do not know, for there is evidence that the German guns were still in action later on, or at least that their accompanying machine guns were, so Legge cannot have

'Legge attacks the guns'. A drawing by Sam Crowder showing D6 and the German battery on Pilgrims Way.

A relic of the world's first tank battle. One of the idler-wheel aperture-covers from Legge's D6, this was found in 1997 when the author and Philippe Gorczynski (who the following year discovered and unearthed an entire tank at Flesquières near Cambrai) were examining the site of D6's destruction. Note that it has a rounded end, whereas in Crowder's drawing this is square. The explanation is that Crowder based his drawing on the Mark II, on which the aperture had been extended, and the cover re-designed, in order to accommodate a longer track-tensioning screw – a modification called for by experience at Flers-Courcelette. The cover measures 9 x 7 inches.

knocked them out entirely. But he must have *thought* that he had done so, even from 100 yards away, for he then turned north again, towards the next German battery – perhaps two batteries – shown on his map, sited on Pilgrims Way. He would not knowingly have left the Bulls Road battery intact, and in his rear, as he crawled ahead at less than one mile per hour to tackle the guns on Pilgrims Way. Had he done so, it could then not only have fired on him north of the road but also continued to fire on British infantry south of it.

He pushed on, hidden at first from his next target but then in full view. He fired one of his 6-pounders and it struck home, destroying a 77mm field gun. But there were three others ready to fire and Legge did not stand a chance. D6 was hit. Seven of her crew scrambled out. 'Lieutenant Legge helped as many out of the tank as possible,' says the War Diary, 'and was last seen standing by the tank.' Three of his crew got back to British lines but Legge was shot and killed, along with two of his men. One man was captured; the eighth man died inside the burning machine.

Reginald Charles Legge had been a Lance Corporal in the 2/1 Buckinghamshire Yeomanry (Royal Bucks Hussars) as recently as mid-March 1916 and joined the Machine Gun Corps after just six weeks Officer Cadet training, but now, in D6 of the Heavy Section, he showed dash and courage of a high order in taking his machine almost to the Fourth Objective, Gueudecourt. He had travelled forward as far as Blowers in D5 but had, like him, found the infantry support lacking in the later stages of the fighting. He was undoubtedly a brave man. 'Dear old fire-eating Legge', said Blowers in later years, 'came very near to being *great*.' He was buried near his tank, possibly by the

FLERS

CEMETERY

Bulls Road. Having kept close to the eastern edge of Flers to protect the men of 124 Brigade attacking there, Legge then dropped down into the shallow valley between the village and what is now Bulls Road Military Cemetery. He advanced along it as far as Bulls Road itself, turned right, then up past the cemetery in order to attack the German battery on the extreme left margin of the photograph. He later turned away to attack the next battery, on Pilgrims Way nearer to Gueudecourt. (TP 1986)

Germans (who returned his will and possessions to London via the Red Cross), but his grave was then lost. His name and those of the men who died with him are now recorded on the Memorial to the Missing at Thiepval.

Second Lieutenant Leonard Bond.

West of the village, Arnold and Bond had taken up positions as specified in their orders. The Germans here had been chased away and during the subsequent lull the crews of D16 and D18 even had time to cook breakfast. But the lull did not last long. German observation balloons had spotted their presence and directed artillery onto them. Arnold moved Dracula around for a period, as a precaution, but Nixon's tank nearby was set on fire, as we know. Some of Arnold's crew left their tank to help put out the blaze but to no avail.

Arnold and Bond, and probably Pearsall

92

View from the south-west. While Hastie entered Flers along the main road from Longueval, Arnold and Bond maintained a parallel course on Flood Street *(le Chemin Blanc)* before advancing up the west side of the village.

as well, were later involved in attacking the German defensive pocket north-west of Flers commanded by *Leutnant* Braunhofer of the 5th Bavarian Infantry Division. The account which this officer left of the fighting makes it clear that the tanks played a crucial role in subduing his position and causing the surrender of all his men.

At about 8.30 a.m. the British had already overwhelmed half of Flers and the southern part of the Flers Line... .A short time after, a tank appeared on the left front of my company position which I immediately attacked with machine gun and rifle fire and also, as it came in closer, with hand-grenades. These unfortunately caused no real damage because the tank only turned slightly to the left but otherwise just carried on. He crossed the trenches in the area of the company on my left, caused us heavy losses with his flanking machine gun fire of trenches which had to a large extent been flattened, without my men being able to do anything against it... .then proceeded in the direction of the road from Flers to Ligny-Thilloy. Positioning himself close to the exit from Flers, he placed the whole length of this road under continuous machine gun fire... .

Well hidden by the houses and buildings in Flers, the enemy advanced into the north and north-west ends of Flers and thereby worked round to our rear. From here and from directly to our left he now attacked, first of all taking the entire length of

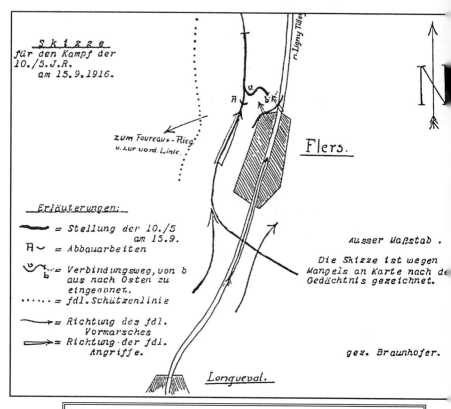

Map 18: A map drawn by *Leutnant* Braunhofer, accompanying his account of the fighting north-west of Flers. Any shortcomings evident in the map can be explained by the fact that he drew it four months later, having in the meantime escaped from a British prisoner-of-war camp and found his way back to Germany. (Bavarian War Archives)

our position under continous machine gun fire and causing more heavy losses to my company... . It was now completely impossible to retreat because all the ground which we might have considered for this purpose was under continual bombardment such that, if we had attempted to withdraw, the rest of my company would have been totally annihilated within a few minutes ... . The Flers-Ligny road and the ground to its east lay under an extremely heavy enemy artillery barrage and were also under fire from the above-mentioned tanks and the numerous enemy machine guns which had been positioned at the northern extremity of Flers.

94

I succeeded in holding out until mid-day. At that time the enemy once more made a mass attack simultaneously from the left and rear (north-west extremity of Flers), this time with even stronger, overwhelming superiority. The attack from the left was led by a tank which, armed with small cannons, came from the flank and fired along our whole position with devastating effect. The attack itself was carried out with hand grenades and bayonets.... Under such circumstances it was quite impossible to hold out any longer; further resistance.... would have led to a completely pointless massacre of the remainder of my company.

It seems that a German counter-attack was later mounted to try to retrieve the position described by Braunhofer. The same tanks were again in action, putting to flight an attacking force advancing across the road which led from Factory Corner to Eaucourt l'Abbaye. At some stage Bond's tank was hit by a shell which damaged its steering and wounded Corporal Paul, the second in command. Bond himself suffered shock, but his role in protecting the infantry of the 41st and New Zealand Divisions was later recognised by the award of the Military Cross 'for conspicuous gallantry in action. He fought his tank with great gallantry, putting a machine gun out of action and capturing the team. Later, he went to the support of a party of infantry, and finally safely brought his tank out of action.'

Arnold, who had picked up an injured New Zealander, was himself wounded while outside the tank by a bullet through the knee. He had then to be rescued by a member of his own crew, Gunner J. Glaister. Arnold, too, was awarded the Military Cross for his work on this day while Glaister, for his part, was awarded the Distinguished Conduct Medal.

We have seen in the previous chapter that an order was issued at 3.30 p.m. calling on the tanks to withdraw in preparation for a resumption of the attack on the following day. This they did (Pearsall excepted) although their inability to fight again so soon quickly became apparent once they had returned to Green Dump.

Although the XV Corps order had also said that no further attacks were to be made until the morrow, it is evident that one was. Among the troops reoccupying positions north of the village was 21/KRRC under their commander, Lieutenant-Colonel the Earl of Feversham, who had gone well forward with his men. For reasons that are not clear he suddenly led his men out into the valley beyond Box and Cox to attack the Germans there. He was shot and killed, as were many of his men.

One possible explanation for Feversham's seemingly irrational act

German prisoners coming in from Flers. Taylor Library

was put forward by Anthony Eden, later Prime Minister but then a subaltern in the battalion. He said that a 'deplorably vague' message was received from 41st Division ordering Feversham to advance to the 'next Objective' but that it had been so long on the way that it was probably drafted when he was still only on the Second Objective. The intention therefore was that he should advance to the Third Objective on Bulls Road, which he had now done, but Feversham believed he had been ordered to attack the Fourth Objective, the Gird Line.

We shall never know for certain the true reason for this tragedy but there can be no doubting Feversham's bravery, nor that of the officers and men who followed him into the valley.

Grave of the Earl of Feversham in Grass Lane A.I.F. Burial Ground.

Field Guide

The tanks allocated to 41st Division assembled north of Longueval, by the junction of the Flers road with the road leading up to the New Zealand memorial (North Street). Groups E and F were to gather on the V-shaped piece of land enclosed by the two roads. Group D was to station itself at the first leftward bend of the Flers road, 300m from the junction. Legge, the sole member of Group C, was another 200m further on still.

The infantry were waiting on either side of the Flers road, above Delville Wood. On the right, stretching across the shallow *Vallée du Bois Robert,* 124 Brigade occupied Green and Brown Trenches, with the leading waves lying out in the fields beyond, finding what concealment they could in the shell holes all around. The rearmost waves found slightly better shelter among the stumps and shattered tree trunks of the wood itself. Ahead, looking down on them all, was the Bank, the *Rideau des Filoires*, with the German front line in Tea Support on its crest.

On the left of the road, the battalions of 122 Brigade gathered in Peach and Tea Trenches and in King's Walk beyond, dug earlier by men of the King's (Liverpool) Regiment. This crossed Flood Street (*le Chemin Blanc*, until recently made of chalk but now asphalted) 75m beyond its junction with the Flers road. Another 75m further still lay

Ruins of Flers village. Taylor Library

the actual front line but 15/Hampshire had withdrawn from here shortly before the opening barrage crashed down ahead of them. The Germans' first line lay astride the highest point of Flood Street, 50m short of the pylon, while 150m due west, where this line was joined by Tea Lane leading over from No Man's Land, is where Bagshaw's tank D15 came to grief. Enoch's D7 had already dropped out, further back.

Returning to the main road you will see that, after continuing for 350m, it now bends round again to the left. On the right is the Bank, known locally as the *Rideau des Filoires*. Its southern end, by the recently constructed irrigation pond, is where Head's D3 finally halted. Nearer its northern end is where Hastie's D17 came to rest after returning from Flers. In between these two points Sergeant Carmichael and the other wounded found shelter under the Bank, surrounded by their dead comrades killed when assaulting Tea Support above them. From here Carmichael looked back at the junction with Flood Street and saw the 'thrilling sight' of the guns and limbers of the field artillery being drawn at great speed by teams of frenzied, frightened horses along the road which you have just come on. (Note that the embankment shown on the trench map as lying north of the *Rideau* no longer exists, having been levelled out many years ago.)

Memorial to 41st Division in Flers.

150m beyond the bend, Tea Support crossed the road. Another 300m further still lay the Switch, where Legge in D6 turned right, before branching onto Gate Lane towards the north-east. Hastie, however, stayed on the main road and advanced to the wire in front of Flers Trench. He crushed this with the weight of Dinnaken's 28 tons then moved over the trench itself – 80m short of the crossroads – where he paused to enfilade the defenders below. Here he was rejoined by the infantry of 122 Brigade, who followed him as he proceeded north, entered Flers, then rounded the double bend (now partly smoothed out) by the church. Here came the infantry – 'the British Army cheering behind' – as he advanced down to *La Place*, now a grass triangle surrounding the memorial to 41st Division. This is where he turned round, finding himself suddenly alone when the German shells began to fall.

Over on the left, Arnold and Bond had eased their way forward along the village outskirts until they emerged onto Abbey Road, the *Chemin de l'Abbaye*. From there they probably drove a short distance down the road to Ligny and took part in the attack on Braunhofer's force. Later still, they helped fight off a counter attack coming from the direction of Factory Corner.

And now poor Legge. From *La Place* take the narrow side road leading down to the east. This is Bulls Road. It leads past the British cemetery of the same name, where a number of men killed in the battle are buried. Follow the road almost up to the crest, beyond which lay the first German battery which Legge attacked and which had just destroyed Blowers' D5 in the field to your right. Having no doubt thought that he had put its guns out of action, Legge here turned into the fields to the north, there to meet his death along with three of his crew. To reach this point, leave your car by the cemetery entrance and walk along the track (shown on some maps as an extension of Fosse Way) which leads to the north-east. This is almost certainly the route taken by the three survivors returning from the stricken D6. After 500m the present track bends right, onto Pilgrims Way, but in 1916 it crossed straight ahead. D6 was hit when just 180m from the crossing, by guns in the enemy battery 200m to your right on Pilgrims Way. The latter, incidentally, was so named because it led to the Shrine, a statue of Our Lady under the trees by the six-way (now five-way) crossroads near Gueudecourt, marked 55 on map 8. The statue is still there.

[i] The witnesses to Legge's will were Bell and Mortimore. The latter had, rather flippantly, given his address as John O'Groat's Farm – an evident allusion to the remoteness of D Company's training camp at Canada Farm, Elveden, where the will was signed.

Chapter Six

16 SEPTEMBER
The Next Day

Most of the tanks used on the first day of the battle were now out of action, either destroyed or ditched or awaiting repair. Only a handful of D Company's machines could be made ready for action on the morrow while none of those in C Company, working with the other corps (XIV, III and Canadian), could be used.

In the area of XV Corps, the available tanks included those of Huffam and Court, who had come to grief at the start point the day before. Pulled out of a trench by men of a Chinese labour company, the machines were found to be unharmed and still serviceable. They were made ready to support the resumption of operations the following day.

Neither commander seemed to know that a third tank was to work alongside them. This was Pearsall's D11, Die Hard, which had stayed forward the day before to protect the New Zealanders from counter-attack. Still up near Flers, its role is not made clear in the records. It was either to help the 'Imperials' on the right of the Ligny road or, more probably, it was to stay with the 'Colonials' when these pushed forward again on the left beyond the village in order to capture Grove Alley.

The New Zealand attack was to be carried out by one battalion of infantry, 1/Wellington. When these had crammed into their assault positions north of Abbey Road and were waiting for Zero at 9.25 a.m., the Germans began their own attack across the ground in front with a force of 500 men. Caught in the open by fresh troops ready for battle, the Germans were cut down in great numbers by rifle and machine gun fire. To this was added the fire of Die Hard's Vickers, as Pearsall began to move down the road to confront the oncoming force and to support

Pearsall's Die Hard outside Flers. The tank in the background is a casualty of later fighting. (IWM)

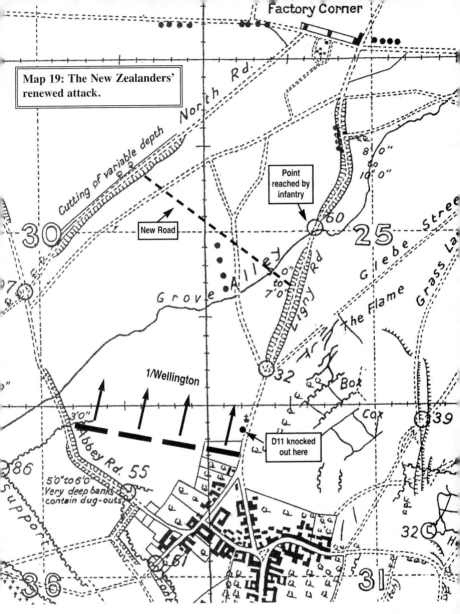

Map 19: The New Zealanders' renewed attack.

Factory Corner

North Rd.

Cutting of variable depth

Point reached by infantry

New Road

30

25

Glebe Stree

Grass La

Grove Alley

Zigny Rd

The Flame

32

Box

1/Wellington

Cox

39

D11 knocked out here

3'0"

Abbey Rd. 55

86

5'0" to 6'0"
Very deep banks
contain dug-outs

Support

36

32

31

the New Zealanders' own forward thrust. Alas, the tank was put out of action by a well-aimed shell which burst underneath it and damaged the gearbox. Pearsall and his men continued to fire their guns, then leapt out to carry on the fight alongside the infantry, now advancing across a field of German corpses. Die Hard's crew had undoubtedly played their part in enabling the whole of Grove Alley to be captured,

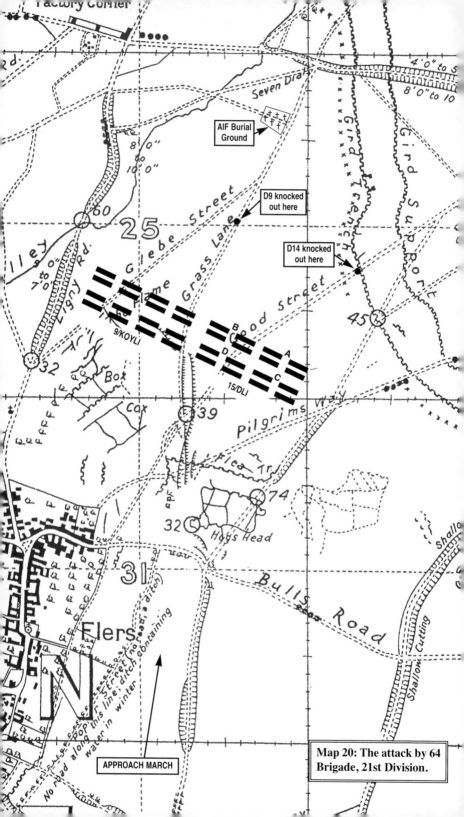

Map 20: The attack by 64 Brigade, 21st Division.

up to the point (marked 60 on our map) where it crossed the road into the area of 41st Division, thus fulfilling the New Zealanders' tasks set by Rawlinson and Haig.

Further east, the infantry prepared to advance to the Gird Line and beyond it to Gueudecourt. Immediately east of the Ligny road, 64 Brigade, attached to 41st Division from 21st Division for the purpose, was to start out from Box and Cox, Flea Trench and the Hog's Head and capture a 1,000 yard stretch of the Gird Line that lay west of the village. However, Brigadier-General Headlam was only told of his brigade's part in this plan at a meeting held at 41st Division's HQ back in Albert at 11.30 p.m. on 15 September. He then had to return to his headquarters at Pommiers Redoubt in order to issue orders to his battalion commanders, which he did – orally – at 1.30 a.m. Written orders were not typed until 5.10 a.m. but they were already out of date, for a report had been received to the effect that during the night British forward troops had had to withdraw to points south of Bulls Road. This, although found later not to be true, caused Headlam to revise his plans and call for 64 Brigade to form up there instead. In the event, the late start, wet weather and slow progress meant that by first light the four battalions, all now very mixed up, were further back still, indeed south of Flers. There they had to halt, and when the time came for them to advance to their assembly positions up by Bulls Road they did so without the benefit that bombardment of the German defences should have conferred. Setting out twenty minutes before the British barrage opened, they suffered from the enemy's shelling and machine gun fire as they made their way across 1400 yards of open ground east of Flers. And when they arrived at Bulls Road and the ground beyond they were surprised to find that British soldiers had been there all the time.

Despite this inauspicious beginning, the attack was put in, 9/KOYLI pushing up on the left and 15/Durham Light Infantry on the right. In support were the two tanks of Huffam and Court. The latter, in D14, went up Grass Lane for 400 yards then branched right, along Good Street. After another 700 yards he found himself immediately in front of Gird Trench. The tank stopped. It would seem that two of the crew were getting out when there was an enormous explosion which annihilated the occupants and left the two others mortally wounded. A German shell had hit home.

Huffam in D9 (Dolly), continuing further up Grass Lane, witnessed the fate of D14 on his right but, unable to do anything to assist, carried straight on. He was now protected by an embankment on his right side but was exposed on his left and front. When just 500 yards from the

Factory Corner, looking east to Gueudecourt. The road leading from Flers toward Ligny and Bapaume winds down from right to left. On this side of it the New Zealanders advanced almost up to the crossroads. Beyond, in the fields between the road and Grass Lane, 64 Brigade of 21st Division managed to make only limited gains, their progress not helped by the disaster befalling Huffam in D9, Dolly, wrecked near the lone trees in the middle distance. (TP 1991)

road running west from Gueudecourt he too was hit, probably by guns at Factory Corner. The shells tore a great hole in the sponson of the tank, killed two of the crew and wounded four of the others including Huffam. The survivors dragged themselves back to the British lines – which were only slightly further advanced than they had been at Zero.

The infantry, wearied by the night march, inadequately briefed about their task and weakened by casualties, had found it impossible to press home the attack and their failure to do so was later the subject of heated debate between 64 Brigade and 41st Division. Efforts to support the assault were made later in the morning but orders were then issued postponing any further attack to 4.30 p.m. Yet further postponement put back the attack to 6.30 p.m. but 41st Division's instructions for this only arrived with Headlam at 5.25 p.m., leaving him no time to organise the operation, which was then abandoned. A chance shell landing on 64 Brigade HQ near Switch Trench had contributed to the delay and confusion, but at least part of the blame for the day's setback could well be laid at the door of 41st Division's staff. At 5.20 p.m. the previous day they had told XV Corps that they had sufficient men available for the attack on the following morning, but at 8.30 p.m. changed their minds and asked that men from another division, the 21st, should undertake the task instead. As we have seen, orders for this to be arranged were not issued to Headlam until 11.30 p.m. and he could not brief his own staff until 1.30 a.m. The cost of this delay was high. In 15/DLI alone, 6 officers and 36 other ranks were killed, 10 officers and 209 other ranks wounded, 3 officers and 174 other ranks missing. Similar delays by 41st Division were responsible for cancellation of the afternoon's attack. Nor did it help to achieve smooth liaison that the division then appointed a relatively junior officer, Major Otter, to be 'commandant of Flers defences' when colonels were already in command of their own battalions there. The appointment was no doubt seen as implicit condemnation of their performance – condemnation made explicit in a critical report on 64 Brigade's performance later submitted by Otter to the division and corps.

On the far side of the corps sector, 43 Brigade of 14th Division, which had taken over from 42 Brigade, was tasked with mounting the main assault on the Gird Line defending the southern edge of Gueudecourt, then capturing the village itself. The initial target given to 6/Somerset Light Infantry was the whole of Gird Support east of Watling Street, their right boundary being on Gas Alley. West of Watling Street were 10/DLI, targetted initially against Gird Support as far left as the point where this was intersected by Good Street (thus

Looking south above Gueudecourt. D9 was destroyed at A, D14 at B, D6 the previous day at C. (TP 1993)

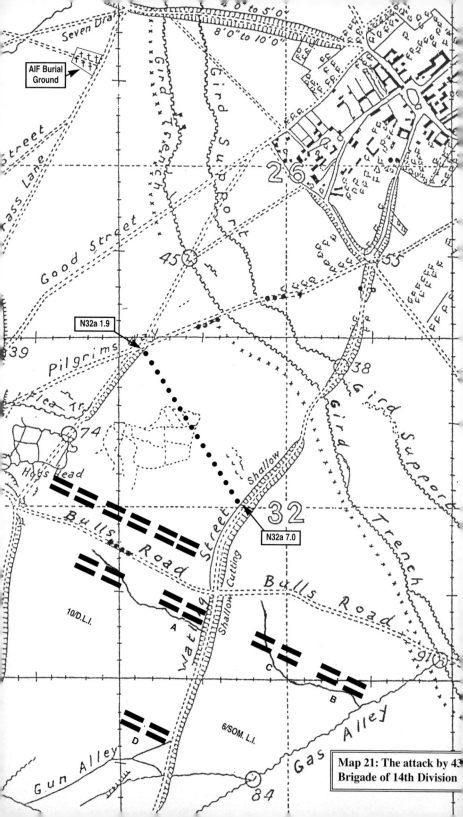

Map 21: The attack by 43
Brigade of 14th Division

overlapping slightly with 15/DLI further left). Both battalions were to have three companies in front, disposed in two waves each of two platoons. In support of the Somerset were Y and Z Companies of 6/KOYLI (W and X had been in action with Mortimore's tank the day before) while all four companies of 6/Duke of Cornwall's L.I. were to support 10/DLI. Their primary task was to occupy the trenches of the Gird Line once these had been seized by the earlier waves, but to remain on call if needed to help carry the assault forward to Gueudecourt and eventually establish a line north-east of the village

Here as elsewhere Zero was at 9.25 a.m., but the day did not go well. A foretaste of the problems to come was given before the attack began. The British bombardment opened about 6 a.m. but it was 'desultory and too scanty to be effective'. A few well directed shots on German troop reinforcements were noted by 10/DLI but before 9 a.m. the guns 'slackened off very considerably and until about 9.15 a.m. few shots were fired. To the left of our line the bombardment had been even weaker.'

As the men of 10/DLI rose from their trenches they were met by a hail of machine gun and rifle fire, some from in front but mainly enfilading from the right.

About 200 yards in front of Bulls Road the ground slopes downwards and to this point the advance was quickly made but with considerable casualties. Entering the dip, the casualties were very heavy, the enemy apparently having the ridge and forward slope well marked down. Before reaching the forward slope the second wave was merged with the first, and the reserve

Reinforcements advancing near Flers, crossing the front German trench captured on 15 September. Taylor Library

company caught up the leading companies at the ridge where they were held up. The barrage during this time was very weak and did not creep forward before the troops.

Some progress was made on the left where we advanced about 200 yards from Gird Trench. Here there was thick wire in front of the trench which had apparently been little damaged. The advance could not be continued further than a line about N32a 1.9 to N32a 7.0. About 9.30 a.m. two platoons of 6/DCLI moved up through an intense barrage and occupied the original front line. At 10.30 a.m. they moved forward but lost heavily and only got half way to our new line.

At 10.15 a.m. 10/DLI reported to 43 Brigade: 'We are held up by m/g fire from Gird Trench in front and from the high ground on our right. The barrage did not creep'. This failure of the creeping barrage to move forward as planned – it either remained stationary or it was too ragged to follow safely – meant not only that the attackers could not advance, but also that the machine guns in front and on the flank were not neutralised. These latter were more numerous; they evidently included those at Point 91, those also in the stretch of Gird Trench to its immediate north-west and those in the short length of Gas Alley still held by the Germans to its south-west.

Given their position, the guns firing on 10/DLI posed an even greater danger to the men of 6/Somerset. At 10.20 a.m. their commanding officer Lieutenant-Colonel T.F. Ritchie reported: 'Suffering heavy casualties from machine guns on right flank.' Further to the rear, 6/Duke of Cornwall's Light Infantry could see the losses sustained by the men ahead and, like everyone else in the area, could see the cause: 'Enemy has intense machine gun fire on right flank which artillery seems unable to cope with.' Several days later Ritchie described what had happened and provided a sketch-map of the ground.

My dispositions were as follows: B Company on the right of A-A trench; C Company on the left of A-A trench; A Company in B-B trench; D Company support in Gun Alley. I had been told the previous evening that I was to attack on the next day and received final orders at about 4.30 a.m. on the 16th. I sent for my O.C. Companies and issued my orders. I do not have a copy but my arrangements were that the attack was to be made in two waves by the companies in the front line. Companies were to right incline on leaving our trench. Company objectives were Gird Support as follows: B Company N33c 4.3 to N33c 1.8; C

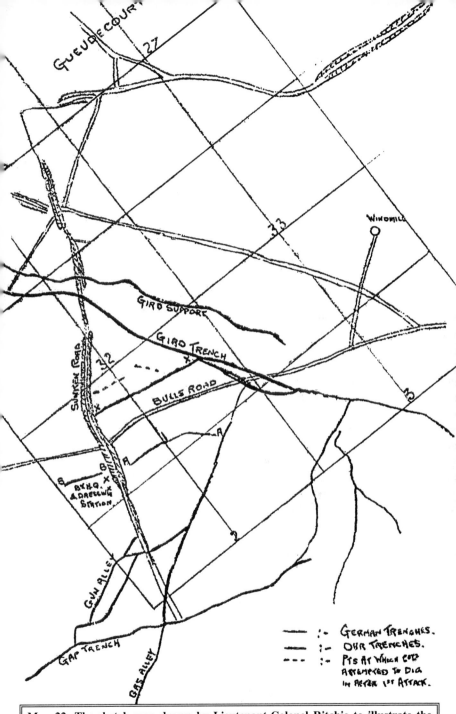

Map 22: The sketch-map drawn by Lieutenant-Colonel Ritchie to illustrate the attack by his battalion, 6/Somerset Light Infantry. (PRO WO 95 1903.) Neither the trench marked A-A nor that marked X-X is shown on GSGS maps drawn up after the battle, although A-A could just possibly be the nearby trench later known as Pen, wrongly drawn. Perhaps both were obliterated by subsequent shelling.

Company N33c 1.8 to N32b 7.2; A Company N32b 7.2 to N32b 3.8; D Company to move to A-A trench at Zero and, when Gird Support had been captured, to Gird Trench. Each company was to leave a clearing-up party of one bombing squad and six men in Gird Trench and then follow the barrage to Gird Support. Both trenches to be consolidated. Zero at 9.25 a.m.

There is a trench which I have called X-X on the sketch. I do not know if it had been occupied by 9/KRRC on the previous day but I imagine not. At any rate, I was unaware of its existence. It is an unfinished German trench. The right end seemed old but a lot of new work had been done on the left and centre. There is a slight ridge between A-A and X-X trenches.

At Zero the men went over but, instead of reaching Gird Trench, the right of B Company reached the right of X-X, the other companies taking the remainder of the trench between this point and the sunken road [Watling Street]. Some six Germans were captured on the right and about a hundred of the enemy ran away. Everyone thought they were in Gird Trench and I was under that impression until the evening. C Company advanced and dug in on a line some 50 yards from Gird Trench. A Company dug in on a line about 100 yards north of X-X trench, with their left on the road. On coming over the ridge between A-A and X-X trenches, the men had come under m/g fire from the north and east and lost heavily. It was impossible for them to advance further. At 9.50 a.m. I received a message from B Company on the right saying that they could not advance owing to the number of the enemy, who were bombing them from Gird Trench. As I had two companies of KOYLI in close support, I sent D Company to their [B Company's] assistance, but on account of the m/g fire they were unable to advance beyond X-X trench.

All companies remained in these positions during the day and I reported that Gird Trench had been taken but that I could not advance further.

I attribute the failure of this attack to the following causes:
1. Insufficient time to reconnoitre the ground in front.
2. Insufficient artillery preparation. Everyone agrees that Gird Trench and Gird Support were practically undamaged.
3. A weak field gun barrage when attacking.
4. M/g fire. This was very heavy and I think came from the following points: Gueudecourt, about N27c central, Gird Trench

at about N32a 8.2 [sic; perhaps N32d 8.2, near Point 91?], *or possibly east of these trenches. Also several NCOs report that there is a strong point or several m/g emplacements about N32b 2.0.*

At 11.55 a.m. Brigadier-General Wood sent a message urging both battalion commanders, Somerset and Durham, to hang on where they were until the situation could be cleared up on their right, where he had just managed to have the bombardment renewed. But doing so had not been easy.

> *Considerable difficulty and delay were experienced in getting* [messages] *through to the artillery as they had to be sent to the divisional artillery and in both cases the line was engaged.*

Meanwhile, further S.O.S. messages were received from the infantry appealing for help. At noon, casualties in 6/Somerset were estimated at 350, including most of the officers. The 10/DLI commander, his men lying out on an exposed forward slope, reported:

> *There is very heavy machine gun fire, probably from shell holes or Gird Trench to our front and right flank and it is impossible to get on. Barrage did not appear intense enough and there was very little of it to the right of the Ginchy-Gueudecourt road* [Watling Street]. *The line of advance is very open and under machine gun fire all the way.*

Then again at 12.15 p.m.:

> *Barrage was not intense enough, especially on the right, and did not search ground in front of Gird Trench in N32 central. Gird Trench in N32d was very little affected.*

And yet again at 1.10 p.m.:

> *I have had very heavy casualties indeed, probably 300 or more, including all the officers that I have heard news of. I must be reinforced...Battalion now back in original front line along Bulls Road. Many stretcher bearers required.*

Finally, at 2.40 p.m.:

> *I estimate casualties at least 400, and believe all company officers are casualties and one at HQ. Believe only three officers left. There are large numbers, I believe, lying in No Man's Land, including several officers. Stretcher bearers are urgently required.*

As Brigadier-General Wood said, communications were partly to blame for the problem. The artillery bombardments of which his battalion commanders were so critical included not only the opening

Stretcher bearers on the way up the line. Taylor Library

barrage, but apparently also the renewed shelling which Wood told them at 11.55 a.m. he had succeeded in arranging. His question to 6/Somerset as to whether it was accurately placed was not answered until 3 p.m. Its ineffectiveness evidently helped shape Ritchie's next decision.

> *At 3.50 p.m. I received a message informing me that the division on our right* [Guards Division] *was to attack at 4.00 p.m. and instructing me to cooperate if I thought there was a fair chance of doing so successfully. I did not think there was such a chance for the following reasons:*
>
> *1. I had no time to make any preparations or to issue orders.*
> *2. The artillery preparation was still inadequate.*
> *3. the m/gs were as active as ever.*
> *I therefore did not attack.*

The extent to which XV Corps was responsible for, or aware of, this proposal for a 4.00 p.m. attack is not clear, but it must presumably be related to the planned 4.30 p.m. attack by 64 Brigade mentioned above. However, corps staff had at 2.40 p.m. already issued its own orders for a renewed assault, now timed for 6.55 p.m. (barrage at 6.30 p.m.) and still to include Gueudecourt village. Wood twice protested to 14th Division HQ that the situation in which his brigade found itself prevented any successful assault being mounted, but he was overruled – although on subsequent reflection the divisional staff, presumably

114

with the permission of XV Corps, excluded the village from the brigade's targets. Ritchie's report continues:

At 6.20 p.m. I received orders to renew the attack at 6.55 p.m., assisted by two companies of 6/KOYLI. After consulting the officer commanding the KOYLI, I arranged that my men should leave X-X trench at 6.55 p.m., the two companies of KOYLI leaving A-A trench at the same hour. I considered that this attack had little chance of success and the short time at my disposal made it impossible for my runners to reach the companies in time for the men, many of whom were lying in shell holes, to be warned. Consequently, when the KOYLI, who advanced at 6.55 p.m., reached X-X trench my men were still there. Most of my companies attempted to advance but the m/g fire was too strong and the attack broke down. I later withdrew all men to the X-X line and, with the assistance of one company of KOYLI, held this line and handed it over as the front line when relieved early the following morning. My losses were 17 officers and 383 other ranks. As every company officer became a casualty, most of them during the first attack, it is probable that either snipers or certain m/gs were told off for this purpose. I also lost a lot of NCOs. The German artillery fire was extremely feeble. During the evening attack they did not put on a barrage and relied entirely on m/gs. Practically all my casualties were from m/g fire. Without a thorough artillery preparation I consider that an attack on this position is unlikely to succeed. The ground is peculiarly well suited to defensive m/g action and the guns are difficult to locate.

On the front of 10/DLI the evening attack went just as badly. Towards the battalion's left the bombardment was better than it had been earlier in the day but its failure to deal with the machine guns in Point 91 and Gird Trench on the right was to leave the attackers, much weakened by the morning's losses, open to further murderous enfilade fire. The three surviving officers, including the Commanding Officer, gathered together all of the sixty available men in Bulls Road, plus a small party of 6/DCLI in support, and then began to advance in two thin waves. To their credit, men who had been lying out in shell holes all day joined them as they passed, bringing the total to 150. But this was not enough. Cut down by enemy fire, now on the left as well as the right, the small force stood no chance of succeeding in its task. The attack was called off.

All 43 Brigade's battalion commanders, including those brought up from the rear to help, were highly critical of the inadequate artillery support which the attackers had been given. Casualties in the brigade were: officers, 17 killed, 47 wounded, 3 missing; men, 140 killed, 769 wounded, 457 missing – in all, 67 officers and 1,366 men.

Field Guide

At Zero on 16 September the men of 1/Wellington were positioned in the fields north of Abbey Road (*Chemin de l'Abbaye*) on the outskirts of Flers. Supporting them from the flank, Pearsall's Die Hard faced down the road leading to Ligny and Bapaume. The place where it was hit was about 120m north of the junction formed by the main road with *Rue du Tourrier*.

To see the ground over which 64 Brigade fought, go down Bulls Road to its lowest point just 300m away. Turn left onto Grass Lane (asphalted as recently as 1996). In the fields to your left 9/KOYLI set out across Box and Cox and marched bravely forward, accompanied on the right of your path by 15/DLI. Glebe Street on the left has now vanished, as has Good Street except for its upper, north-eastern portion.

Continue along almost to the cemetery and you will see a group of trees by an embankment on your right. Huffam's D9 (Dolly) was destroyed here, its wreck lying half on the road and half in the field to your left.

Spare some time to look at the cemetery, the Grass Lane A.I.F. Burial Ground, for as well as the Australians who later fought nearby, it contains the bodies of men killed on 15 and 16 September 1916, including that of the Earl of Feversham.

Now move out onto the main road and turn right, into Gueudecourt. Turn right again along the right side of what used to be the church and go up to the gates at the top. Do not enter them but turn right, then left, eventually coming out into the fields. In the line of trees to your left were positioned the German 77mm guns which destroyed Court's D14.

Walk down the track, Good Street, for 320m, in other words to a point 100m beyond where it bears slightly left. You are now standing on Gird Trench, where the disaster occurred.

One of the best vantage points from which to survey the right wing of the British attack on 16 September is, unsurprisingly, Point 91 where machine guns were sited that caused horrendous casualties among the officers and men of 14th Division and the Guards on 15 and 16 September – let alone among the troops who fought here later on. To reach it, take the *Chemin des Guilmonniers* out of Gueudecourt and follow this for just under one kilometre. Bear

Gueudecourt church photographed in February 1915.

left at the fenced-off pond and drive up the road for 650m, noting as you do that this runs roughly parallel to part of Gird Trench on your left (shown as Needle Trench on later maps). At the top, where the road bears left to Les Boeufs, is where Point 91 was sited, its position here – at the top of where the eastern portion of Bulls Road used to run – dominating the ground over which the British tried to advance. Below you, running from the road near the field boundary on your left and roughly in line with the western end of Delville Wood, was Gas Alley ('Rut Lane' on later maps), the top 100m of which were stubbornly defended by Germans determined to prevent the capture of their vital strong point. The section of Bulls Road which once led up towards you on Point 91 has now been ploughed under but the 'slight rise' between the trenches marked A-A and X-X on Ritchie's map is clearly visible. In the middle distance, the western part of Bulls Road, lying nearer to Flers, has now been asphalted. In 1916 its banks were deeper and on 16 September they formed the front line sheltering the men of 10/DLI as they waited for Zero.

Chapter Seven

17-24 SEPTEMBER
The Interval

The next few days following the operations of 15 and 16 September were devoted mainly to reorganisation and consolidation, and planning the next phase of the battle. Proposed originally for 18 September, this was later postponed to 21 September because of increasingly wet weather. The urgent need to re-supply the hungry guns and the need also to synchronise plans with the French to the south, caused yet further postponement and it was not until 25 September that renewed movement on any scale became possible. In the interval, 14th Division was relieved by the 21st, and 41st Division by the 55th, both of the newcomers then carrying out minor, but often costly, operations.

On the left, the New Zealanders had stayed in the line and indeed had spilled over their left divisional boundary to help the neighbouring 47th (2nd London) Division who, following the trauma involved in capturing High Wood, were now much weakened. On 15 September they had been unable to reach their Third and final Objective which lay along 400 yards of Flers Support (south-east from point 66 on our map), but had managed to seize most of it, in pouring rain, early on the 18th. The one place still not in their hands was the vital junction of Flers Trench and Flers Support with Drop Alley, leading up from the south-west, and with Goose Alley, dominating the crest to the north-east.

The New Zealanders later took over the manning of Flers Support, leaving the Londoners in Flers Trench and Drop Alley. Neither division was closer to the junction than 100 yards but in bloody fighting late on 19 September men of both divisions attacked with bomb and bayonet and narrowed the gap to 40 yards before the Londoners were driven back. The junction was finally taken on 20 September following an attack in the darkness at 8.30 p.m. by a small force of bombers from 1/Black Watch of 1st Division advancing up Drop Alley and by three companies of 2/Canterbury approaching Goose Alley in line abreast from the lower ground on its south-east side.

But the 13/Bavarian Reserve were not ready to leave matters there. At 10 p.m. they counter-attacked in force and pushed back both the Black Watch and the larger Canterbury force until the New Zealander Captain F. Starnes rallied the defenders and led them forward again, just before dawn, to eject the attackers. The whole episode was

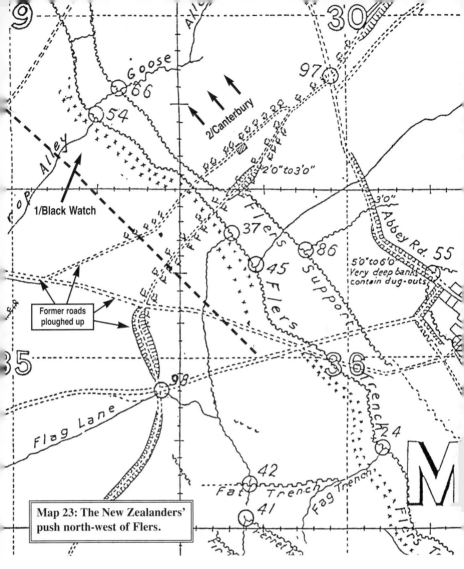

Map 23: The New Zealanders'
push north-west of Flers.

repeated in the afternoon of 21 September, when a determined attack
by fresh German units was pushed back yet again, this time for good,
by men led once more by Captain Starnes.

From Goose Alley XV Corps could now look down into the
Eaucourt valley and observe much of what the Germans there were
engaged in.

On the corps' right, it was recognised that the enemy machine guns
around Point 91 still posed a major threat, so at 4.30 p.m. on 18
September an attack up the adjacent Gas Alley, preceded by an intense

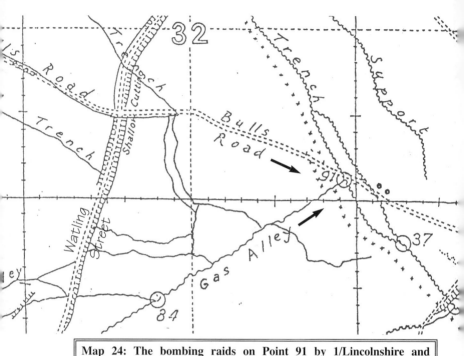

Map 24: The bombing raids on Point 91 by 1/Lincolnshire and 13/Northumberland Fusiliers.

artillery bombardment, was mounted by a bombing party of 13/Northumberland Fusiliers (62 Bde of 21st Division). This failed, partly because of determined opposition, and partly because, as the Fusilier commander later complained, the part of Gas Alley occupied by the Germans was completely undamaged by the bombardment. The brigade's Bombing Officer, who witnessed the whole operation, thought that no British shell had landed nearer than 200 yards from the target.

On 20 September a second attack was made, or rather two attacks mounted from separate places, one up Gas Alley again, the other up the trench alongside the eastern portion of Bulls Road. Both were to be protected by a barrage provided by the Corps heavy artillery, but this was 'most inaccurate and did practically no damage to the enemy, many of the shells falling in our front line along Bulls Road'. In consequence the bombing parties, consisting of 1/Lincolnshire and 13/Northumberland Fusiliers, suffered heavy casualties.

When attacking up Bulls Road, the British found that the upper portion of the trench leading to Point 91 had ceased to exist and that they were consequently obliged to attack over the open. Several attempts were carried out but all failed. In Gas Alley, the British removed their own barrier, erected earlier against possible German counter-attacks, then advanced up the trench to remove the one erected by the enemy. Having done this, they continued up the trench for 100 yards before a German party threw them back. Nothing daunted, they returned to the attack and advanced again up to, and this time just 50 yards beyond, the German barrier. In all, the line had been moved only 70 yards. It is a measure of the importance attached to this spot that even the Army Commander, General Rawlinson, spent time on the following day debating the Gas Alley problem with his senior staff.

Field Guide

To see the area where the New Zealanders fought, take Abbey Road (*Rue de l Abbaye*) leading west out of the square in Flers. Just before the water tower, turn left and walk or drive 550m – crossing Flers Support then Flers Trench as you do – to where a new (or much realigned) road leads right. The lower portion only dates from the 1995 *remembrement* which regrettably saw also the elimination of several of the ancient trackways nearby. Follow this road for 700m up to the point where it bears slightly left. On your right there was until recently a useful landmark, a field boundary, roughly aligned with the poplars visible in the distance. If crops and the season allow you can walk along this line for 150m, then north and northwest for a further 100m to the junction of trenches so bitterly fought over. Alternatively, walk 100m beyond the bend in the road and then turn right along the course of Drop Alley. A walk of 150m will bring you to Point 54 on our map. There is nothing to see, except what you see in your imagination.

For the attacks on Gas Alley go to Point 91, described in the previous Field Guide.

Chapter Eight

25 SEPTEMBER

On 25 September the tasks facing the men of 21st and 55th Divisions were substantially those remaining unfinished from 15 and 16 September, which for them included attacking and capturing the Gird Line and Gueudecourt itself. South of the village were 64 Brigade and 110 Brigade of 21st Division, the two brigadiers sharing a headquarters in Hastie's D17, Dinnaken, abandoned on 15 September under the *Rideau des Filoires*. To the left of their battalions stood those of 165 Brigade of 55th Division, while further left again stood the New Zealanders, still occupying ground wrested from the enemy since the battle began, but ready and eager to expand their hold by further bold attacks.

64 Brigade were assembled east of Watling Street, up against the

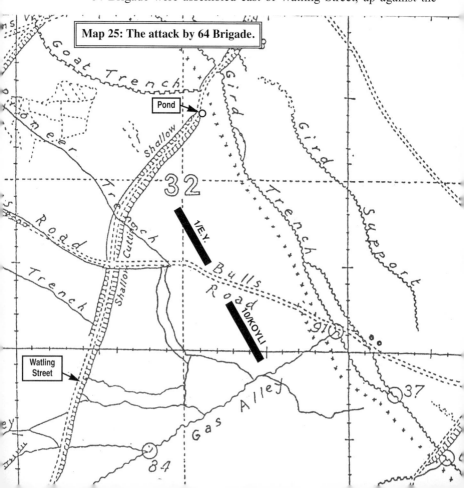

Map 25: The attack by 64 Brigade.

divisional boundary, the Guards being their neighbours. On the right were 10/KOYLI and on the left 1/East Yorkshire, no doubt heartened to learn from night-time patrols that the wire in front of Gird Trench had been successfully destroyed. At Zero, 12.35 p.m., the men stepped bravely forward but immediately came under intense machine gun fire, especially from the right. Reports on their progress were confused. One said they had entered Gird Trench, another that they were in Gird Support beyond it. Then an aircraft of the RFC reported that Gird Trench was packed full of Germans – news which alarmed Brigadier-General Headlam, who feared that the enemy had worked down from Gueudecourt village and was now placed between the front wave of British attackers and their supporting troops, an extremely dangerous situation.

In fact none of this was true. The enemy in Gird Support had simply lit flares of the kind that British infantry employed to signal their position to their own aircraft, the German intention being to keep British artillery off them, and at the same time to encourage the attackers to approach both Gird Trench and Gird Support over open ground in the belief that they were free of the enemy. The ruse might have been even more successful had the British been free to move. Instead, they were pinned down in front of Gird Trench before wire which, despite those original reports from patrols, was virtually intact. It had been hidden in a hollow and could not be seen from the British lines by day nor, apparently, detected by patrols at night. The men stayed in front of the wire until nightfall. 10/KOYLI alone had lost seven officers and 43 other ranks killed, with many more wounded or missing.

On the left of Watling Street, the men of 110 Brigade had reached their jumping off trenches by 2.30 a.m. They arrived there with only little loss from the enemy's night-time shell fire, although casualties began to mount thereafter. The 9/Leicester on the right and 8/Leicester on the left were to lead the attack from New Trench (later called Pioneer Trench) but were dismayed to find that this was only a shallow scrape barely twelve inches deep. Nonetheless they were cheered by those same optimistic patrol reports about the state of the German wire. During the night they fired frequent bursts of machine gun fire across No Man's Land in order to prevent the Germans carrying out repair work on their defences.

When daylight came, everyone kept their heads down as best they could to avoid the enemy discovering just how many British troops were crammed into the area, but at Zero, 12.35 p.m., when the assaulting troops went 'over the top', the Germans were ready. They immediately opened a heavy artillery barrage across the whole front and in great depth, causing severe casualties.

The Leicesters had planned to attack in eight waves, with two platoons from each battalion in each wave. Men in the first waves were

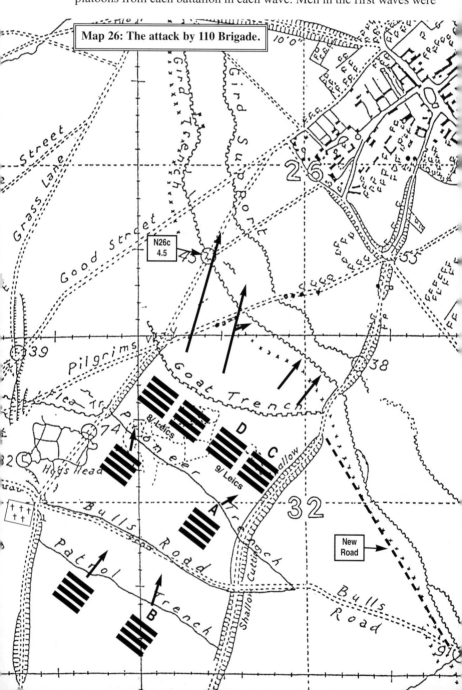

Map 26: The attack by 110 Brigade.

among the first to fall, but despite this the survivors captured Goat Trench – recently dug by the Germans – with little opposition from the occupants, then went on to seize part of Gird Trench. But as they did so, they came under a new threat posed by heavy machine gun fire from the right flank. This came mainly from the part of Gird Trench still occupied by Germans on the rising ground lying between Watling Street and Gas Alley, and in particular from the gun or guns at Point 91 which had inflicted so much damage ever since the battle opened on 15 September. Survivors from the first two waves of 9/Leicesters' C and D Companies now occupying Gird Trench to the north-west of this part, i.e. west of Watling Street, were in consequence subjected to enfilade fire of devastating intensity. Only very few of the third and fourth waves coming up behind were able to reach their comrades further forward so the remainder formed a defensive flank by dropping into Watling Street and facing east up the slope where the enemy lay. The men of A and B Companies, intended as reinforcements, were unable to get through, so established themselves in New Trench (Pioneer Trench), Bulls Road and Patrol Trench. When Captain Allberry later made a further attempt to lead A Company forward he and many of his men were immediately killed by machine gun fire from the right flank.

Men of 8/Leicester, further left, were a little more fortunate; some of their first two waves, together with a number from their third and fourth waves, succeeded in getting into Gird Trench whilst some, according to a claim in the battalion's War Diary, went further:

> They then pressed on to their Second Objective which was the village of Gueudecourt. By the time they reached the village their ranks were sadly thinned, by the tremendous artillery barrage the enemy put up and by machine guns which wrought terrible havoc. Nevertheless, with dauntless gallantry they pressed on, reaching the village and engaging the enemy in hand to hand fighting which took place all the night. In the morning the 7th Battalion relieved the 8th in the village and the enemy were finally driven out.

The Official History seems to doubt this story ('If this be true, they were not seen again.') but concedes that other reports did refer to British troops being seen in Gueudecourt at this time. Such reports caused divisional HQ to believe for a while that the village had been captured. But it had not.

In their advance beyond Goat Trench the 8/Leicester had gradually veered to the left and had allowed a gap to form between themselves and 9/Leicester. On realising this, those who had reached Gird Trench quickly formed bombing parties to work over to the right, but German counter attacks, which were already ejecting 9/Leicester from that part of Gird Trench which they had succeeded in occupying, now barred their way. Indeed, they began to push the British back along the trench but were stopped some distance short of N26c 4.5 where the Leicesters set up a block.

Alas, the efforts of the leading waves of both battalions had been of only limited value to their comrades further back, now advancing from the south. The successive waves of both battalions were stopped by the fire in front and to the right and sought shelter in the sunken roads on either side, Watling Street and Fosse Way. Four platoons of 6/Leicester, coming through in support, managed to reach Pioneer Trench but the remainder found themselves bunching up in the trenches lining Bulls Road.

When planning this assault on Gueudecourt, XV Corps had counted on the assistance of two tanks which it was hoped would breach the German defences around the village. However, one of the machines had become ditched in Flers and the difficulties subsequently experienced by the infantry in getting forward threw grave doubts on the wisdom of using the surviving tank alone. Later, confronted by the problems posed by Point 91 and the Germans still in the Gird Line nearby, XV Corps decided to use this machine in order to clear the trench once and for all. It was only with difficulty and repeated pleas that the commander of 21st Division, Major-General Campbell, managed to persuade his Corps Commander that the men were in no fit state to provide the necessary support for the enterprise. The plan was postponed to the morrow.

On the left of 110 Brigade stood 165 Brigade of 55th Division. Its first task was to seize Gird Trench and Gird Support lying west of the village and as far north as the road leading west from Gueudecourt, together with the stretch of road itself running towards, but not quite as far as, Factory Corner. Once this Objective had been reached, the attackers were to capture the remaining portion of the road leading back into the village. At 12.35 p.m. the men of 7/, 6/ and 9/King's Liverpool Regiment rose up from their trenches and followed their officers forward over the open ground. On the left, 9/King's kept close behind a superb creeping barrage, having formed up in four waves at 100 yard intervals, with bombers on each flank. These dealt with the defenders still left alive in the strong points encountered in Grove Alley, but not before a number of casualties had been suffered. On the

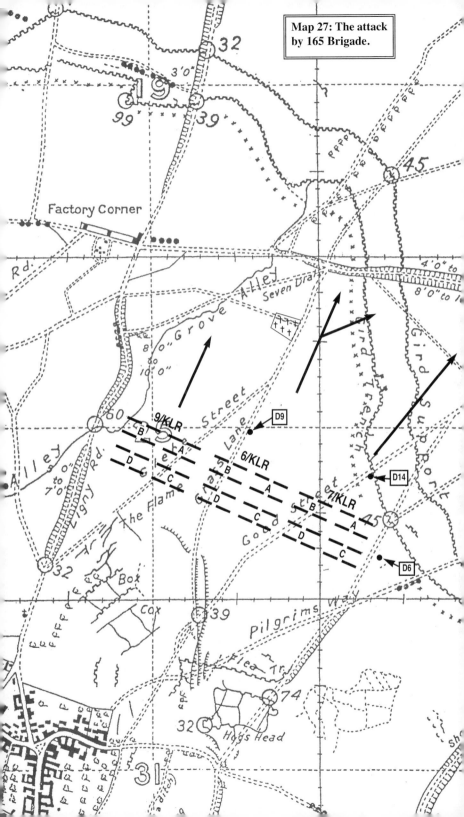

Map 27: The attack by 165 Brigade.

right and in the centre, 7/ and 6/King's would have passed the wrecks of three tanks (Legge's D6, Court's D14 and Huffam's D9), but there was no time to pause. Many prisoners were taken but the price was high, both in officers and men killed or wounded. Nonetheless all three battalions reached their targets by 1.00 p.m. At 2.40 p.m. 7/King's and part of 6/King's continued their advance to the Second Objective, while the rest of 6/King's crossed the road to place a block in the trenches continuing north.

Further left, the New Zealanders were to push north-west from Grove Alley to a line running between Factory Corner and the Goose Alley spur, eventually joining up with the Flers Line at a point just above its junction with Goose Alley. They attacked in magnificent fashion, with 1/Canterbury on the right, 1/Auckland in the centre, and 1/Otago on the left. They swept first of all into North Road then, after a pause, up to Goose Alley and the high ground of the spur. The dash and vigour of their assault may have been one reason why their casualties on this occasion were comparatively light.

Elsewhere the day had cost the men of XV Corps much blood and hardship. It was perhaps some comfort, not only that the New Zealanders had done well but also that the neighbouring XIV Corps (5th, 6th and Guards Divisions) had this same day captured Morval and Les Boeufs.

German prisoners being searched at a 'cage' in the rear.

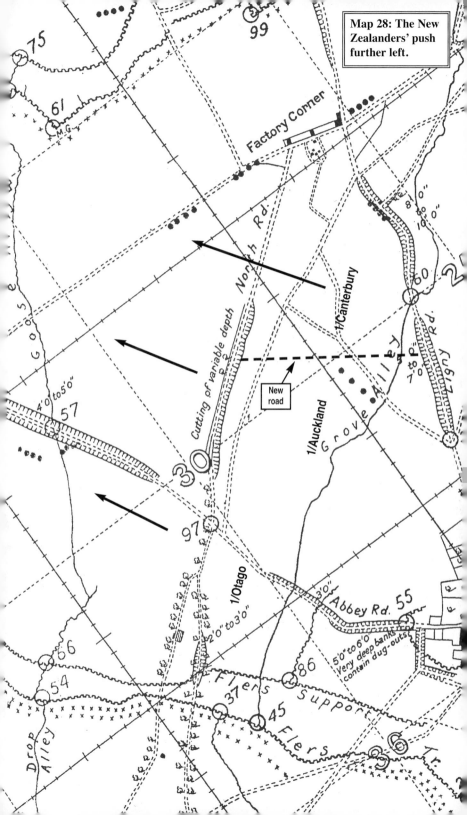

Map 28: The New Zealanders' push further left.

Factory Corner

75

61

L.MG.

99

North Rd.

1/Canterbury

60

Cutting of variable depth

New road

1/Auckland

Grove Alley

57

4'0 to 5'0

30

97

1/Otago

2'0 to 3'0

30"

Abbey Rd. 55

5'0" to 6'0
Very deep banks
contain dug-outs

66

86

54

37

45

Flers Support

Drop Alley

Flers Tr.

Field Guide

Again, the best place from which to survey at least the right wing of the British attack on 25 September is Point 91 where machine guns were sited that were reckoned to have caused 80% of the casualties among the officers and men of 21st Division – let alone those of the Guards and 14th Divisions on 15 and 16 September. To reach it, follow the directions given in previous chapters. On our map of 64 Brigade's action we have not shown the new road which climbs up from the enclosed pond beside Watling Street because to do so would obscure the wire which proved such an obstacle to 10/KOYLI and 1/East Yorkshire. But note that for the first one third of this road both the wire and Gird Trench lie several metres to your left, although they draw progressively closer to you. For the centre one third you are on top of the wire, and for the last one third Gird Trench lies immediately on your left and actually reaches the road at Point 91. As you climb this gentle slope look down onto the fields below you, bisected in 1916 by the eastern section of Bulls Road. It was here that the Yorkshiremen advanced and here that so many died.

Of course Point 91 provides a good view of the area of 110 Brigade but to see this close to, go down again to the pond (which lies only a short distance from the eastern end of Goat Trench) and turn left along this asphalted section of Watling Street. It was here that some of C Company of 9/Leicesters, unable to reach their comrades in Goat Trench and Gird Trench, dropped down from the fields above to face the enemy guns to the east. But now continue south to the crossroads and turn right, into Bulls Road. This runs more or less parallel to the Leicesters' jumping off positions in Pioneer Trench 150-200m to your right, but is also where many of the casualties were brought back to, during and after the fighting. Continue over to Bulls Road Cemetery, where you could well spend some time, then perhaps walk up the rough track (shown on some maps as a prolongation of Fosse Way) which goes north-east. This was the left boundary of 8/Leicester and leads on to Pilgrims Way, where you are nowadays obliged to bear right. Another 250m brings you to Gird Trench, where fierce bombing fights took place.

To view the area fought over by 165 Brigade, drive to the lowest point of Bulls Road and turn right, following Grass Lane all the way to the Gueudecourt-Factory Corner road, as described in Chapter 5. It was in the fields on either side of this that the men of Liverpool advanced.

The New Zealanders' area of operations can be viewed from a number of places: the Factory Corner-Eaucourt road, Abbey Road as far up as the Goose Alley spur, or from the new access road (*chemin d'exploitation*) linking the Ligny road with North Road.

Chapter Nine

26 SEPTEMBER

Early on 26 September a new tank D4, again commanded by Second Lieutenant C.E. Storey, moved out of Flers along Good Street (or Pilgrims Way, the record is not clear) and took up position on Gird Trench. It had been delayed by the poor state of the ground but it now turned right at the block erected by 8/Leicester at N26c 4.5 and began its slow progress along the German-held portion. Closely followed by a bombing party of 7/Leicester under Second Lieutenant Walsh, supported further back by C and D Companies of that battalion carrying a supply of 1,000 grenades, Storey enfiladed the whole trench with his Vickers guns. The occupants began to move swiftly away, down the trench towards the south, gathering in numbers as they went. Some chose to seek shelter in the dugouts but were ordered to come out, the alternative being grenades tossed in by the Leicesters lining the parapet and parados. Many others scrambled up ladders and tried to make a run for it but were immediately shot down. Others were killed by bullets from an RFC aircraft flying low overhead. Meanwhile the flood of men now jamming the trench moved ahead as fast as their comrades further on would allow. They pressed on, pursued by the monstrous apparition breathing death and fiery terror from its sides. The spectacle was extraordinary.

There was a temporary check at Watling Street where the tank plunged down the bank onto the road below, but Storey then carried on for another 200 yards before turning off to the left, heading towards Gueudecourt village. He must have concluded that the operation was going smoothly enough, which it certainly was, for the bombers carried on with no check at all. Some of the defenders surrendered to the

A later posed photograph illustrating the effect tanks had on the German lines.

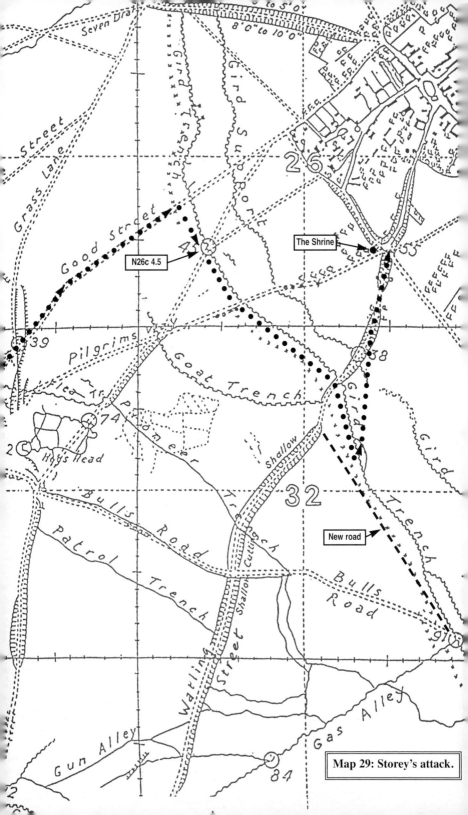

Map 29: Storey's attack.

Leicesters on the spot but most simply moved up the trench in a long stream until they emerged, ironically at Point 91, near which the Guards Division were waiting to escort them back to the prisoner-of-war cages.

Storey, whose first tank had ditched in Delville Wood on 15 September and who had taken no further part in the battle that day, had now proved in spectacular fashion that the new weapon of war could bring success to those who used it well. He and his crew had been instrumental in capturing eight officers and 362 men and in killing many others now left in the trench or in the fields around it. The Leicester casualties were two killed and two wounded. This was surely a just revenge for the slaughter of the British below Point 91.

What now happened to Storey is unclear. The War Diary of his own unit, D Company of HSMGC, says simply that he returned because he had run out of petrol. He may have done, but not yet. Otherwise why would he have headed away from base and towards the enemy still in Gueudecourt? Almost certainly he thought he still had work to do, as indeed one eye-witness testified. Major C.A. Milward, second-in-command of 10/KOYLI who had watched Storey's progress down Gird Trench with evident wonder and admiration, approached Gueudecourt himself later on and said:

> *We heard from the tank man who had returned, covered with blood and bound up, that he had crawled his tank over the*

Storey's route seen from the north-west. (TP 1991)

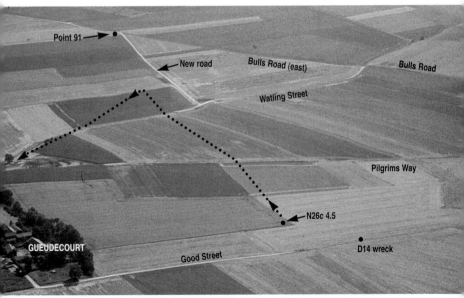

*village and, instead of meeting fifty Germans as expected, he had
come across five hundred whom he had taken on. In the end he
had run out of petrol but had managed to get back himself.*

We do not know Storey's route into and through Gueudecourt but to
have engaged 500 of the enemy there, with few if any infantry to lend
him support, is surely a measure of Storey's courage, but his other
exploits on this day had already earned him a place in the history of
warfare for he had saved dozens if not hundreds of British lives. He
had, however, paid a price, he himself being badly wounded in the eye
and four of his crew being wounded by 'splash – molten lead from
bullets hitting crevices in the armour – and by the hot splinters of steel
flaking off the interior of the tank whenever it was hit by machine gun
fire on the outside. Given the circumstances, Storey was right to head
home but on its way back through the British lines his tank had to be
abandoned. All eight men returned to Flers.

The collapse of opposition in the Gird Line evidently convinced the
Germans that the village itself was no longer tenable. They withdrew
northwards, their positions in Gueudecourt being taken before noon by
infantry patrols gradually filtering in from 64 Brigade. Later, cavalry
patrols from the South Irish Horse and 19/Indian Lancers were sent
round the east side of the village but were heavily shelled when they
neared the far side. Other cavalry units, dismounted, entered the
village, as did elements of 110 Brigade who dug in on the north side
as the cavalry withdrew.

All XV Corps' targets were now won.

The ruins of Gueudecourt after the battle.

Field Guide

The south-western end of Good Street has now disappeared, so to see where Storey's tank began its historic journey, go first into Gueudecourt. Drive up along the right side of what used to be the church and go to the gates at the top. Do not enter them but turn right, then left, eventually coming out into the fields. Walk down the track (this is the north-eastern end of Good Street) for 320m and you are standing on Gird Trench, at a point which you have already visited in order to see where Court's D14 was hit. At a distance of 130m on your left (roughly south) lay D4's start point at N26c 4.5. The tracks in its immediate vicinity have long disappeared, so depending on the season and on the crops you may or may not be able to follow the course of Gird Trench at this point. Note however that it swung south-eastwards before crossing Pilgrim's Way, then Watling Street (*Chemin des Guilmonniers*) just 100m north of the pond and road junction described in earlier chapters. There is a considerable drop here, which must have given a bit of a jolt to the commander and crew of D4. Nothing daunted, they continued up the further stretch of Gird Trench for 200m before turning back towards Gueudecourt. Presumably Storey then made for the Shrine crossroads but we cannot follow his route thereafter. Point 91 has of course already been visited.

Chapter Ten

EPILOGUE

The Battle of Flers-Courcelette had been conceived as a major offensive designed to sweep through the German lines on the Somme, principally on the front of XV Corps, but broadening out to engage the enemy across a larger area, enabling British forces to effect a deep penetration of his forces to the north. The battle was seen as an infantry operation, supported as usual by the other arms of artillery, aircraft and eventually cavalry, but this time also by tanks. This was their first use in war and among some military figures much was expected of them. Others remained sceptical.

No doubt both proponents and opponents thought their views vindicated by the outcome. The tanks had not achieved a decisive success against the Germans. They had suffered a number of setbacks, including mechanical weaknesses, insufficient training and inadequate tactical planning, but above all an inability to cope with the hideous terrain – a battlefield almost everywhere covered by shell craters – for which they had not been designed. Infantry who had looked to the tanks to provide an easy way through the defences in their path were understandably disappointed wherever the promise remained unfulfilled.

Many, however, at all levels, saw the potential of the weapon. Even Haig, so often accused of being wedded to outmoded methods of war, retained that enthusiasm for tracked armour with which he had greeted news of its appearance back in January. Only three days after the battle began he sent his Deputy Chief of Staff, Major-General Butler, to London to plead for a thousand tanks to be manufactured as soon as possible. On that same day, 18 September, he wrote in his diary about his discussions with Admiral Bacon on the subject of landings on the Belgian coast:

> In view of the successes obtained by the tanks, I suggested that he should carry out experiments with special flat-bottomed boats for running ashore and landing a line of tanks on the beach with the object of breaking through the wire and capturing the enemy's defences... [and] I asked him also to urge the loan of personnel from the Navy for manning one hundred tanks.

In all this Haig provides convincing proof that, at least in the matter of armour, he had far more imagination than the great Earl Kitchener, who earlier in the year had grudgingly conceded that just six tanks might be manufactured.

Much has been written about Haig's decision to use the tanks at a time when so few were available. Swinton had urged, in his earliest paper on the tanks, that they should not be used 'in driblets', for instance as they were produced by the factories. In this he was supported by Churchill. Both men had argued that an attack should be postponed until such time as we, and our allies the French, had sufficient numbers in hand virtually to guarantee success. But such arguments were open to question. Even if the secret of the tanks' existence could have been kept (which is doubtful) until, say, the spring of 1917, success at that stage could not have been guaranteed. By the end of that year, armoured tactics, tank design, and cooperation between arms were still not sufficiently developed, despite the experience gained in various tank engagements (Arras, Ypres and even Cambrai). To have gambled everything – men, machines and the credibility of the weapon itself – in one vast operation earlier that year would have been folly. The Germans would have prepared their defences on an equally large scale. The result in London and Paris of failure on the battlefield would have been bitter disappointment.

But on the battlefield of the Somme in 1916, those infantry who had benefitted from the tank's presence were elated by its success and saw it as a 'war-winning weapon'. It may not have been, at least on its own, but its existence on the battlefield in 1916, 1917 and 1918 undoubtedly contributed to the success won by all arms – infantry, artillery, aircraft, cavalry and tanks – culminating in the final Advance to Victory. Perhaps the tank crews themselves would reply that the greatest achievements in the Great War were those of the infantry who fought alongside them, without whom nothing could have been achieved. The truth, of course, is that *all* should be honoured.

Ruins of Flers.

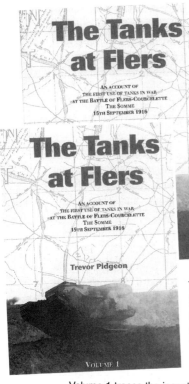

If you have enjoyed this book why not also read...

THE TANKS AT FLERS

ISBN 0952517523
by Trevor Pidgeon

AN ACCOUNT IN TWO VOLUMES OF THE FIRST USE OF TANKS IN WAR AT THE BATTLE OF FLERS-COURCELETTE, THE SOMME, 15 SEPTEMBER 1916

Monstrous machines, lumbering into battle for the first time in the history of war - 'reptiles of steel', 'toad-chimeras', 'terrestrial whales' - the Mark I tanks of the Somme caught the imagination of the world.

Their story and that of the men who manned them is told for the first time in this highly detailed, two-volume work. Meticulous research in the British and German archives and painstaking study of the ground where the battle was fought have combined to make this the definitive account of that epoch-making event.

Volume 1 traces the inception and construction of the first machines, the selection and training of the crews, their arrival in France and their launch into the bloodbath of the Somme. Individual chapters are then devoted to their work with each of the ten divisions involved in the fight, which stretched from Combles in the east to Courcelette in the west, while the Field Guides take the reader along almost every yard that the tanks themselves covered.

Volume 2 forms a wallet of twelve large-scale maps, mostly at 1:10,000 (about 6 inches to the mile), being black and white copies of original British trench-maps, overlaid in colour to show the trenches, battle lines, objectives and tank routes.

✦ ✦ ✦ ✦ ✦

The Daily Telegraph: A fine example of self-published military history....Trevor Pidgeon recounts a powerful, although sombre tale....It borders on the incredible that it has taken until now for someone to perceive and rectify the absence, right through eight decades, of a tank-by-tank account of that day.....[What marks this book] is quality. It is the quality that comes of devotion, unstinted effort to suit the presentation to the subject.....[Its maps are] nowadays almost unthinkable treasure.

Stand To! (Journal of the Western Front Association): A masterpiece... Never before have I been at such a loss for superlatives to describe a book as I am, now, in the case of this outstanding publication...Individual chapters are devoted to each division, and the fortunes of the tanks fighting with them are described in meticulous detail with the help of the relevant trench map, which not only traces the progress of each tank in the battle, but also shows the British positions down to company level. Supporting this are aerial photographs in colour of the battlefield today, breathtaking in their clarity and definition, also annotated to describe or pin-point movements and positions....There are a number of features about this book which deserve special mention. First, the book itself, a handsome production, attractively set out on high quality paper, very easy to read and exceptionally well written. Then the photography, the marvellous contemporary shots of individuals, groups and tanks on the battlefield, and the superb colour photographs which include exterior and interior shots of the Mark I provided by the Tank Museum at Bovington. Thirdly, the maps, and these are the royal icing on the cake. Fourthly, the meticulous attention to detail and care for accuracy which is evident throughout. And last but by no means least, the value for money is unsurpassed by anything I have ever seen. Even if you are deciding never to buy another book on the Great War, make sure you get this one first.

The Army Quarterly and Defence Journal: Pidgeon has produced a work of loving scholarship...He has not merely recorded the battle, he has recorded the movement of single tanks, having mined the archives to find RFC photographs in order to follow individual tank tracks. His present-day aerial photographs, all in colour, with battle detail superimposed, give a real feel for the ground 80 years ago, and his maps - 12 separate ones in a companion folder - make walking the battlefield today effortless.

Tank (Journal of the Royal Tank Regiment). One of the most scholarly, well researched and interesting books on the detailed history of the first use of tanks in war...augmented by beautifully clear, overprinted reproductions of contemporary mapping.. and by a wealth of colour and black and white photographs.....Trevor Pidgeon's account not only covers every aspect of this fascinating story from an historical perspective that is breathtaking in its detail and depth of research, but also offers, at each stage of the account, a proposed battlefield tour, supplemented by modern (often aerial) photographs overprinted with position markers. It is, by any standards, a splendid piece of work that I commend most highly.

Armor (Journal of the US Army's Armor Center): Pidgeon's work is the most complete and comprehensive account of the tank's battlefield debut yet published..The Tanks at Flers is superbly illustrated with photographs and drawings from the period......It is a unique account of a long ignored aspect of the First World War and the development of armoured warfare.

Military History (U.S.A.): Arguably the most comprehensive book currently available on the subject, The Tanks at Flers is an important addition to the library of any serious student of armored warfare - after all, this is where it all began.

The Literary Review: Trevor Pidgeon, through massive research in official histories and war diaries, has written the authoritative account of how tanks fared on their first day on the battlefield. His industry and command of detail leave one gasping. [It is an] important contribution to the history of tank warfare.

British Army Review: Sometimes a book comes along where all the reviewer ought to say is, quite simply, "this is one to buy". The Tanks at Flers is one of these.

Visit **www.tankbook.com**

INDEX

Abbey Road 66,69,101,103,116, 121,130
Admiralty 8,20
Allberry, Captain C.C. 125
Arnold, Lieutenant A.E. 71,78,80,92, 95,101
ASC (Army Service Corps) 21,42,48
Asquith, Right Hon. Herbert 8,20
Bacon, Vice-Admiral R.H.S. 136
Bagshaw, Lieutenant J.L. 74,78,80, 100
Baskett, Captain R. 83
Bavarian Reserve Regiment 118
Bell, Lieutenant H.R. 74
Below Stellung 61
Below, General Fritz von 61
Bernafay Wood 38,49,52,53
Big Willie 21
Bisley 25
Blowers, Second Lieutenant A. Ch.3 *passim*, 90,101
Bond, Second Lieutenant L.C. 10,74,78,80,92,95,101
Bouleaux Wood 30
Bown, Second Lieutenant H.G.F. 59,60,66,67,69
Braunhofer, Leutnant 65,93-95, 101
Brewery, the 35,37,38,40,44,52,53
Bronfay Farm 49
Brown, Sergeant Donald Forrester,VC 59
Brugère, General 10
Bulls Road 44,46-48,54,89-92, 101,105,116,117,120,125,130
Burton Park, Lincoln 20

Butcher, Lieutenant C.E. 61
Butler, Major-General R.H.K. 136
Campbell, Major-General D.G.M. 126
Carmichael, Sergeant N. 77-80, 87
Cavan, Lieutenant-General Lord 35
Charlesworth, Major W.H. 40
Chimpanzee Valley 51
Churchill, Winston Spencer 8,20,136
Cooksey, Second Lieutenant P.T. 83
Court, Second Lieutenant G.F. 73,74,102,105,116,128,135
Crucifix Alley 52
Darby, Second Lieutenant H. 59-63,66,69
Debenham, Gunner W. 65
Delville Wood 35-42,47,48,53-55,71,77,78,99,117,133
Die Hard 67,68,102,116
Dinnaken 67,82,85,86,100,122
Dobson, Rifleman J.W. 61
Dolly 105,106
Dolphin 37,47,48,55,90
Dracula 74,92
Eden, Lieutenant Anthony 98
Elderfield, Sergeant 45
Elveden 25,101
Enoch, Lieutenant A.J. 74,100
Factory Corner 61,67,68, 70, 95,101,106,126,128,130
Feversham, Lieutenant-Colonel The Earl of 95,98,116
Flers Riege l61

141

Flood Street 78,93,99,100
Foden, Corporal E. 48
Fork, the 59,60,69
Fosse Way 54,101,126,130
French, Field-Marshal Sir John 20
Frost, Gunner R. 61,62
Gallwitz Riegel 30
Glaister, Gunner J. 95
Glebe Street 70,116
Good Street 105,116,131,135
Grabenzug 46,47,55
Grass Lane 70,105,116,130
Green Dump 51,52,57,69,71,95
Grovetown 50,51
Gwyn-Thomas, Major G. 84
Haig, General Sir Douglas 8,21,27,30,34,105,136
Hankey, Maurice 19,20
Happy Valley 50,51
Hastie, Lieutenant S.H. 67,73, 78,80,82,84-86,100,122
Hatfield 21
Head, Second Lieutenant H.G. 40,42-44,53,54,86
Headlam, Brigadier-General H.R. 105,107,123
High Wood 30,53,56,61,66, 69,118
HLI (Highland Light Infantry) 67
Hohlwegzug 45,46,55
Horne, Lieutenant-General H. 35
HSMGC (Heavy Section of MGC) 21,133
Huffam, Second Lieutenant V. 73,74,102,105,106,116,128
Hutchinson, Jim 80
Kidd, Corporal 79
Kitchener, Field-Marshal Earl 9,19,136
Kohl, Leutnant 45

Legge, Second Lieutenant R.C. 73,78,80,89-92,99-101,128
Lejoindre, Georges 10
Little Willie 20
Loop, the 33,49-51,53,71
Marten, Lieutenant-Colonel C.P. 78
MGC (Machine Gun Corps) 21,91
Milward, Major C.A. 133
Mitchell, Lance Corporal 79
Mortimore, Captain H.W. 10,37-42,44,49,53,109
National Rifle Association 25
Nixon, Captain G. 59-61,63, 65,69,70
North Road 128,129
North Street 59,69,99
Oakley, Lieutenant-Colonel R. 84
Otter, Major 107
Paul, Corporal 95
Pearsall, Second Lieutenant H.G. 59-70,92,95,102,103,116
Pfister, Georges 10
Pilgrims Way 91,92,101,130,131,135
Plateau Line 50
Point 91 110,113,115,117,119-121,125,126,130,133
Pommiers Redoubt 105
Preliminary Operation 35,37,38,52
Rawlinson, General Sir Henry 27,30,33,56,105,121
Remembrement 54,55
Rideau des Filoires 99,100,122
Ritchie, Lieutenant-Colonel T.F. 110,115,117
RNAS (Royal Naval Air Service) 21

Rodgers, J. 59
Russell, Major-General Sir A.H. 57
Sellick, Captain S.S. 74
Shrine, the 101,135
Staddon, Lieutenant W. 83
Starnes, Captain F. 118,119
Stern, Albert 21
Storey, Second Lieutenant C.E. 41,53,131,133-135
Swinton, Lieutenant-Colonel Ernest Dunlop 9,19,20, 33,136
Thomas, Private G.H. 48
Tritton, William 23
Vallée Raison 49-51
Walsh, Second Lieutenant H.J. 131
Watling Street 44-47,54,55,107, 112, 113,123,125,126,130, 131,135
William Foster & Co 21
Wilson, Walter 23
Wood, Brigadier-General P.R. 113,114
Young, Private B.J. 66

British Units
Guards Division 114,117,123
1st Division 118
5th Division 128
6th Division 128
14th Division Ch.3 *passim*,71, 107,108,114,117,118,130
21st Division 105-107,118,122, 126,130
41st Division 61,65,66, Ch.5 *passim*,105-107,118
47th Division 66,118
55th Division 118,122,126
New Zealand Division

Ch.4 *passim,* 118,121, 122,128,130
41 Brigade 36,37
42 Brigade 107
43 Brigade 107,108,116
62 Brigade 120
64 Brigade 105,106,114,116, 122,130,134
110 Brigade 6,122-124,126, 130,134
122 Brigade 71,76,83,84,90, 99,101
123 Brigade 71
124 Brigade 71,74,83,84,89, 92,99
165 Brigade 122,126,127,130
Auckland Regiment 57,128
Black Watch 118
Buckinghamshire Yeomanry 91
Canterbury Regiment 118,128
Duke of Cornwall's Light Infantry 109,110,116
Durham Light Infantry 105-117
East Surrey Regiment 76,83
East Yorkshire Regiment 123,130
Hampshire Regiment 76,79, 83,100
Indian Lancers 134
King's (Liverpool) Regiment 126-130
King's Own Yorkshire Light Infantry36,40,105,109, 112,115,116,123,130,133
King's Royal Rifle Corps 35,36,41-45,76-79,83,93,112
King's Shropshire Light Infantry 44,47
Leicestershire Regiment 6,26,123-126,130-133
Lincolnshire Regiment 120
New Zealand Rifle Brigade 60

Northumberland Fusiliers 120

Otago Regiment 57,128

Oxfordshire and
Buckinghamshire
L.I. 44

Queen's Royal West Surrey
    Regiment 74,84

Rifle Brigade 35,36,41-45

Royal Fusiliers 74,83,89

Royal West Kent Regiment
    76,79,83

Somerset Light Infantry 107-114

South Irish Horse 134

South Lancashire Regiment 74

Wellington Regiment 102,116